Military History of India

Military History of India

By

SIR JADUNATH SARKAR, Kt., C.I.E.

GYAN

Published by

Gyan Publishing House
5, Ansari Road
Daryaganj, New Delhi-110002
Phone: 011-47034999, 9811692060
E-mail: books@gyanbooks.com

Distribution Network
gyanbooks.com
India, USA, Canada, UK, Australia, France

ISBN : 978-81-212-6806-6 (PB)
First Published, 1960

2nd Impression 2022

Printed at: Gyan Press, Delhi.

MILITARY HISTORY OF INDIA
Author: SIR JADUNATH SARKAR

MILITARY HISTORY
OF INDIA

SIR JADUNATH SARKAR, KT., C.I.E.,

HONORARY MEMBER, ROYAL ASIATIC SOCIETY OF GREAT BRITAIN

WRITER'S NOTE

This series is a study of the development of the Art of War in India, and not a descriptive list of every battle that has been fought in our land. Only such battles are discussed here as can teach a military student what to do and what not to do. Mere skirmishes, panic flights without striking a blow, rebellions and riots are outside the scope of this study Sieges and naval fights will not be treated here.

CONTENTS

Chapter I

HOW GEOGRAPHY DICTATES STRATEGY

Basic Facts[1]

The general principles of war in their basic truth are the same in all ages,—namely, how to get at the enemy's armed force, crush it, and thus destroy that people's will to continue the war. Civilisation changes with time and the weapons of war change with advancing civilisation. But wars are always decided by three cardinal factors:

First—the *Terrain* for both strategy and tactics;

Second—the *character* and mental development (miscalled race) of one people compared with their opponent's; and

[1] What is the practical use of the study of the history of past warfare to a soldier of today? Is it an idle diversion of his mind or an unprofitable act of pedantry? No; for if it were so, an intensely practical nation like the English would not have founded chairs of military history (like the Chichele Professorship at Oxford), nor made the military historian a necessary member of a Staff College. The Navy is the senior service in Great Britain, and the importance of military (in which term I include naval) history in its proper functioning is thus clearly set forth in a recent issue of the *Times* (Lit. Supplement, May, 30, 1952) in discussing the life of Sir Herbert Richmond, an experienced admiral and erudite scholar, who may well be called "the Mahan of England." The *Times* writes:

The Navy, he thus came to realize, existed as an instrument of war; and it therefore behoved its officers to learn how to use it in that capacity. Finding no guidance in that direction from the Admiralty or senior officers, he turned to "History, not as an end in itself, but as a means of learning something about strategy" (as he wrote later). And having absorbed many lessons on matters of principle which history had to teach, he sought by discussion and argument with his brother officers to apply those principles to the actual conditions of this developing mechanical age and to evolve a theory of war for their present guidance.... Seeing clearly the need to evolve a doctrine of war if the Navy's effort was not to be misdirected and wasted when the test came, Richmond was an enthusiastic advocate of the creation of a Naval Staff. (This was done by Mr. Churchill in 1912 and Richmond was appointed to it as Assistant Director of Operations next year. The World War came on 4th August, 1914).

This is a civilian's sufficient apologia for venturing into this field. Here is a practical necessity why the wars of India in the past ages should be studied by the soldiers and sailors who are to defend the free India of today.

Third—the difference in arms and equipment between the two sides. This last includes organisation and trained leadership. No doubt, the genius of a "heaven-born general" can overcome many of the difficulties in these respects, but such geniuses are a rare gift of fortune to a nation, and we cannot normally count on them.

North Indian Plains

A look at the map of India will at once explain to us how geography has laid down some inexorable laws for the time and manner of conducting military operations in our country. First note the basic difference between Hindustan and the Deccan, that is, the lands respectively north and south of the Vindhya range. In any school atlas of India, we see a green belt shaped somewhat like a horse-shoe, stretching north-westwards from Calcutta by way of Patna, Allahabad, Delhi to Lahore and then southwards to Karachi. This is the fertile plain of India. From Calcutta to Lahore the distance is 1,300 miles and yet the difference in height above sea-level between these two cities is only a thousand feet, or in other words the ground rises only nine inches in one mile of road.[1]

The next features, to strike our eye on the map of India are the yellow patches of dry plateaus and deserts, whose colour fitly suggests sand and bare rock, treeless for most part of the year. Cutting these are many black lengths of the hills,—the Himalayas guarding the entire north, with the Sulaiman Range closing the north-western frontier down to the Arabian Sea, the Vindhya (and in a more broken shape the Satpura Range with their outcrops like the Kaimur hills) running west to east and dividing the peninsula in the middle. The short and low Aravali Range running diagonally borders the Sindh-Rajputana desert and overlooks the plain of Agra-Delhi at its northern end.

[1] This would not be surprising in the Bengal Delta, but a thousand miles upcountry from Calcutta, the ground formation is the same in the Delhi district: "The river Jamuna enters this district at a height of some 710 feet (at the north end) and leaves it at about 630 feet above sea-level, with a course within the Delhi limits of rather over 90 miles and an average fall of between ten and eleven inches to the mile." (*Delhi Gazetteer* of 1883-84, p. 3).

Deccan Hills

In the Deccan proper, the Western Ghats protect the entire western coast as a long wall parallel to the Arabian Sea, while the more broken Eastern Ghats do the same thing but in a lesser degree to the vast Eastern Karnatak plain. From the Sahyadri Range in the west with its continuation the Anamalai Hills in the extreme south, spurs run eastwards into the plateau, like ribs from a spinal column; and between every two such spurs flows a stream collecting the rainfall of its bordering hills and carrying it down to the Bay of Bengal as a vast many-branched ever-widening river, the great Godavari, Krishna and Kaveri.

Thus Nature has cut the Deccan up into many small isolated compartments, each with poor resources and difficulty of communication with its neighbours. Hence, invading armies are slowed down in their march in such a terrain and usually starved out even when they have penetrated to any of these nooks.[1]

These Deccan hill ranges, particularly the Sahyadri, are often crowned by lofty forts, towering above the lowlands on some cliff with steep scarped sides and artesian water supply on the flat top or sides. These forts are Nature's gifts to which the people can retire for safety when defeated in a pitched battle in the plain below. From these shelters nothing could expel them before modern artillery, if only they had laid in provisions or could smuggle in food at night by the back door.

Therefore, the North Indian plains have been generally the seats of vast empires, under monarchs claiming to be universal suzerains and reducing their neighbours to feudatory vassalage. The Deccan, on the contrary, except for a few

[1] A north to south advance in force is impossible in most parts of the Deccan, as Napoleon found in Spain, in which Peninsula, exactly like the Deccan, long parallel mountain chains (called *sierras*) run west to east, cutting the country up into isolated districts, and an army from France after crossing the Pyrenees can reach any city in the south only after painful climbing up and dismounting from several parallel hilly barriers on the way. The command of the sea alone enabled the English to easily transport their troops to any part of the Spanish-Portuguese Peninsula by landing in either the east or the west coast ports and following the valleys between the *sierras*.

short periods, has been divided into small isolated kingdoms, each confined to its own corner and unable to present any united opposition to a foreign invader. Vast cavalry forces can easily sweep—as they have done age after age in the past—through the green belt from the Khaibar Pass via Delhi to Bengal's capital, without meeting with any natural obstacle, if the forts on the way are by-passed. In these plains, empires have fought empires, and India's fate has been decided by one single gigantic clash of arms. Not so in the Deccan; here the national resistance can be, and has often been, more obstinate and successful.

Campaigning Season

The physical geography of India has also dictated the campaigning season. There can be no movement during the three months of rain, 15th June to 15th September. The rivers are then in high flood, the roads are turned into mud pools, and the fields are submerged, with the higher villages standing up like islands surrounded by a sea of water.[1]

Every year when the rainy season ends with the month of September, the river levels fall, and the crops ripen, the invasion begins. Ancient Hindu tradition, followed by the Marathas almost to our own days—only obeys geography when it prescribes the Dasahara day, early in October, as the auspicious time for a king to set out on conquest, *dig-vijaya.* In a month or so the crops are being harvested, so that the invaders can live off the country without burdening themselves with supplies. The herbage has not yet been blasted by the summer sun, so that their elephants and horses can get green fodder. And the falling river level enables them to cross the rivers by fording them at the upper reaches of the streams flowing down from the Himalayas—at Rupar, Buria-Mustafabad, Hapur &c. —without having to build bridges of boats or lose time on the bank.

A force of practised horsemen, mounted on the superb

[1] The early English travellers wrote of our monsoon season as winter, from its likeness to the season of rain snow and hail storm in England.

horses of the Khurasani or Iraqi breed, marching in a compact body of 8,000 men (like the army that brought Babur to Delhi) or 24,000 men (like Ahmed Shah Durrani's own troops at Panipat)—could make a rapid dash through the level green belt, skirting the foothold of the Himalayas and reach Delhi without a halt. The Indian infantry, and even our cavalry mounted on country-born small ponies, could not come up quickly enough to bar the enemy's path, and if they gave battle, they were hopelessly defeated, because infantry cannot manoeuvre with the speed of cavalry; while mounted troops can at will avoid hand to hand fight with an enemy advantageously posted or in superior numbers, or wheel round and attack some weak spot of the Indian line of battle. The invader's superior mobility bewildered the Indians and frustrated their previously formed plan of operations; the cities lying behind the fighting front could not be defended against enemy forces that made a rapid detour round the main Indian Army facing the frontier.

CHAPTER II

ALEXANDER AND POROS: SOCIETY & ARMY CONTRASTED

The fight between Alexander and Paurav (326 B.C.) is the first Indian battle of which we have any description written by men practised in the art of observing things in an objective scientific manner and recording them with accuracy. But this record is from one side only; the other party do not appear at the bar of history, not even through later traditions.

But to us Hindus, the reports of Alexander's campaigns in the Punjab have an absorbing interest, because they show us—though in broken glimpses and not as a complete picture—the state of society and Government among the descendants of the Vedic Aryans who had come to colonise that province during the preceding ten centuries. We know of Aryan society as it was in the north-west about 1000 B.C. (the central date of the collection of the Vedic hymns), and we also know of Hindu society as it was in the North Indian plains in the age of Samudra-gupta and Kalidas (say, 375 A.D.), but nothing with precision about the period between them. The Greek writings help us to light up this dark gap in our knowledge of our forefathers' life, though in a fragmentary manner.

What picture do we get here of the society and government of the descendants of the Aryans who had passed in stream after stream for centuries through the Punjab to Mathura and Ayodhya, Kashi and Pataliputra, leaving behind them a string of colonial settlements in the Land of the Rivers? The first thing that strikes us is, that there was as yet no vast single empire, but only a multitude of small States—*Khandarajya* in Sanskrit,—some under petty kings, but most others tribal republics or village communities each living in isolated local independence.

Every king had his immediate neighbour as his enemy, and that neighbour's enemy as his ally. Even his own kinsmen were not always his friends; the younger sons of a king had no profession except to conquer some fresh territory, or when that was not possible to cut up the parent kingdom into principalities of their own. Paurav's own nephew was in rebellion against him, and he had to be subdued with Macedonian help after Paurav had made terms with Alexander. The creation of these apanages by younger sons was a perpetual source of domestic feud, as we see among the Rajput clans seventeen centuries later. The political solidarity of a vast kingdom or empire with consolidated sub-kingdoms, compact boundaries, powerful resources and a strong integrated defence organisation, was wanting, and hence the military weakness of the scores of small units which chequered the political geography of the Punjab.

The mass of the people were not combined into one common nation. Each colony represented only one group of immigrants left behind in the wake of the Aryan push to the east, or some pre-Aryan aboriginal tribe that had survived the shock of Aryan conquest and stood like an island amidst the sea of Vedic settlements in the land. Every such settlement lived an isolated self-sufficient life like a trade guild or small sept (*i.e.*, sub-division of a clan, in the course of time hardening into a new caste). The Indian tribe that the Greek called *Oxydriki*, I take to mean Shudras or non-Aryans living outside the pale of the Vedic social system. Alexander found no district in the Punjab with a geographical name, but all were known by the names of their ruling tribes, *i.e.*, the name of the tribe with the plural suffix *an*, such as *mousik-an*, and even in the middle ages *Jhang-i-Sialan* or the city of Jhang colonised by the Sial tribe.

Alexander found some kingdoms but many cities in the Punjab. Each city was walled round and conducted its defence by means of mercenary soldiers who lived in it and were noted for their bravery and fidelity to their employers. This was also the policy of the city republics of Italy in the later middle ages.

Sometimes the community was larger. A number of cities all inhabited by one tribe such as the Malavas (Greek, *Malloi*) and their subject aborigines formed one State, with rivers on their two sides helping them to stand forth as a clearly marked geographical unit, but no such natural boundary separated them from another tribe lower down in the same *doab.*

The Greeks called these tribal republics or village communities, "independent", that is, kingless. The Sanskrit name for such political units *aratta* (A-rashtri) appears in the Greek writings in the form of *adraisti* or *aratroi.* These tribal republics, though patriarchal in their ancient origin, were now without any patriarchal head and could be more correctly described as baronial oligarchies with no king over the barons. The nearest parallel to their polity was that of the Sikh *misls* in the same region in the late 18th century, before the rise of Ranjit Singh who fused the *misls* into one kingdom and made the Punjab unconquerable by the Afghans. Such was not the happy lot of that province in the age of Poros. Divided we fell.

The Punjabi warriors are described by the companions of Alexander as darker and taller than the other Asiatic peoples they had met with, and the bravest enemy they had ever encountered. Is not this a forecast of the Sikh soldiery, born of the same Jat race?

No Buddhist was encountered in the Punjab in Allexander's time; all the people were Hindus and image worshippers like the Greeks themselves.

They marched to battle carrying before them as their standard the image of Hercules. It is clear that by this the Greek writers mean Krishna and not Balaram, whom the Greeks identified with their god of wine Dionysos—Bacchus. Megasthenes likens him to the Theban Hercules, whose emblem was the eagle, corresponding exactly to garuda, the bird of Krishna. Garuda-topped standards were presented to Samudragupta (c. 350 A.D.) as his Allahabad pillar inscription records.

The Brahmans (translated into Greek as philosophers) were priests by profession, and had cities of their own in the Multan district and southwards. Though they no longer fought like their Vedic ancestors, they were inspired by the same lofty spirit; they roamed about the country inciting the people to resist the foreign invaders, and turning the public contempt upon those princes who had joined the Mlechcha conqueror. For this Alexander regarded them as his chief enemies and hanged many of them when he caught them, besides massacring the population after storming any city of the Brahmans. (Plutarch)

This disunited, narrowly self-centred, mainly rustic population had to oppose the greatest General of the age, at the end of his unbroken series of victories from Greece to the gateway of India. Empires like the Persian, martial tribes like the Afghans and Turks, sea and desert, forest and rock alike had failed to arrest his progress. Macedonian soldiers, originally trained and hardened in battle by his father, had been turned into a body of matchless veterans under his own banners in a series of stiff fights from Asia Minor to the Swat Valley.

In the Middle East, the kings subjugated by him had sent contingents of their best troops to serve under him. The most valuable fighting material among the mercenary tribes of western Asia had been hired by him. Thus the army that he led against Poros had not only a core as hard as adamant, but was also strengthened by light forces of many races which enabled him to vary his tactics at every corner of the battlefield.

Above all shone the resplendent genius of the greatest Commander of men that the antique world had produced, able to knit together all these diverse elements and make them obey one will. The perfect co-operation of all the branches of his army in the battlefield ensured his victory, and that co-operation could be so prompt and faultless only as the result of discipline practised for years before. No tribal levy, improvised for national defence under the threat of invasion, can show this solidarity.

In the first written description of a battle between Asiatics and Europeans, the Ionian father of song has noticed their difference of character which had the most decisive influence on their fighting capacity. This battle was joined on the shore of the Dardanelles, where Asia faces Europe: As it started, "The Trojans marched with clamour and shouting like birds, as when there goes up before heaven a clamour of cranes which flee towards the ocean. But on the other side, the Achaians marched in silence, breathing courage, *eager* at heart *to give succour man to man*" (Iliad, book ii, A. Long's translation). The Indian defenders of the Punjab were brave, but each man fought to the death in isolation, exchanging blows hand to hand and unable to make a mass movement in concert with their brethren of other corps.

And the brain of the Macedonian army was made up of the most learned men among the greatest civilised nations of the ancient world. Alexander himself was Aristotle's pupil, and he carried in his train Greek philosophers, scientists, doctors, engineers, catapult-workers, and mechanics who could take to pieces 30-oared galleys, transport them by land and quickly join them together to float on the river eighteen miles away. There were also an efficient staff-corps, transport organisation and intelligence service. Besides, many Indian spies were lured by money to bring him news of their own side.

When we come to compare the arms and equipment on the two sides, we feel as if men of the Bamboo Age were fighting men of the Steel Age.

The army that Alexander took with himself was originally the creation of his father, Philip of Macedon. "It was Philip who first created a national army on a broad basis not only of cavalry and infantry, but of archers and all kinds of light-armed troops, so that he had at his disposal many mobile elements which could be used in a great variety of ways in conjunction with the heavier phalanx". (Cambridge Anc. History, vi 206).

Invading Army

The elements of Alexander's army:—

COMPANIONS:—The companions (Gr. *Agema*) of the Sovereign, or personal guards of the King, were the most esteemed arm of the Macedonian army. It consisted of choice cavalry and the sons of the nobility were enlisted in it. This corps enjoyed the first place in the army like the Household cavalry of France and the Guards of England. "At the beginning of the campaign this body consisted of 1,500 men, but in the course of the war their number was increased, perhaps to 5,000 (McCrindle, 57 n.). Rider and horse were cased in armour.

HYPASPISTS:—The title means "bearers of the round shield", as distinct from the *hoplites* who carried oblong shields. They were mercenaries and used as heavy infantry, but as they were not so heavily armed as the hoplites, they were more rapid in their movements. Their spears were shorter, their swords longer and their armour lighter than those of the phalanx. The *agema* or royal escort, contained the corps of royal foot-guard, to whom the Hypaspists were joined.

HOPLITES:—Heavy infantry; they had formed the backbone of the famous Spartan army. They wore armour, and carried a sword, a spear, and an oval shield, which covered the whole body. Well-trained, well-equipped, densely massed for fight, they often proved irresistible.

PHALANX:—This was the most notable element in the Macedonian army. The soldiers wore full defensive armour, *viz.*, a helmet, a breast-plate, and two long curved plates (greaves) protecting the thighs but not covering the lower legs. Their arms were a long sword (four feet), a long shield, and distinctive spear called *sarissa* (like our *barssa* but in name only). This spear was 24 feet in length and weighed at six feet from its butt-end, so that when balanced in the soldier's hand at that point, it projected 18 feet before him. Hence, the spearheads of the next six ranks, each standing three feet behind, projected in front of every soldier of the first line. As the phalanx charged, it presented the appearance of a gigantic porcupine, or a moving forest of seven successive rows of glittering steel points. The *chevaux de frise* and *abbatis* of modern Europe were not so deadly an obstacle and they were pinned down to one place.

Philip reduced the formation of the phalanx to sixteen deep. When a man in the front ranks fell, a fresh soldier from the 8th or still hinder ranks (who used to hold their spears uplifted for freedom of movement) rushed forward to fill the vacant place, so as not to let the column lose its compactness and uniformity. Philip's object in making the phalanx a less dense mass than the usual Greek hoplite infantry, was that it should give up the old policy of "carrying the day by sheer weight, but get room for a more skilled play of weapons and keep the enemy's front engaged, while the other troops won the victory by freer movements". (CAH. vi 205).

ARCHERS:—Alexander had bodies of mounted archers and javelin-men. They were light-armed and very useful for skirmishing and harassing the enemy ranks from a distance. In addition to Thracian and Thessalian light cavalry called *Agrianians,* he had also Scythian archers enlisted in Asia. These oriental archers (when they entered the Roman service a few centuries after Alexander's death) are described as "mainly cavalry, armed with the *most dreaded weapon* of antiquity, the composite bow of the Iranian and Turkish nomads." [Camb. A.H. xii. 216.]. "These archers shot equally well dismounted and at the gallop,... and their missiles pierced cuirass and shield with ease." (*Ency. Britn.,* 11th ed., ii. 363).

ARTILLERY:—Gunpowder was then unknown, but Alexander's engines, called *Ballists* and *Catapults,* worked by the hand, threw stones and darts to the distance of 300 yards, and often proved very effective in his sieges.

In the Indian Army there were:—

(i) *Chariots*:—This was the proudest arm of the Indian forces, and a *Rathi* enjoyed the honour of a knight in Medieval Europe. Each chariot was drawn by four horses, and carried six men, namely, a shield-bearer and an archer on each side, and two drivers armed with javelins. When the chariot could not move and the fighting was at close quarters, the drivers dropped the reins and hurled dart after dart against the enemy. But these cumbrous wooden structures had to be built heavy in order to carry six men and their arms. They could not move fast like our one-horse *ekkas* or two-horse *tangas,* which are two-wheeled and of light structure.

In the battle with Alexander, the Indian chariots proved to be of hardly any use, as the heavy and incessant rain of the night before had turned the ground into a marsh and the chariots kept sticking in the mudpools, immovable by reason of their enormous weight. When the drivers lashed the horses to make a move, the excited animals only overturned them into the mud. Some cars in the course of fast driving were overthrown by the treacherous sodden surface of the field. (Q. Curtius.)

(ii) *Infantry*:—The Indian infantry was variously armed, most of them with bows and some with javelins, but many carried sword and shield only. Megasthenes thus describes them. "The Indian infantry have a bow equal in length to the man who carries it. Placing this down to the ground and stepping against it with the left foot, they discharge the arrow, drawing the string far back. Their arrows are little less than three cubits long, and nothing can withstand one shot by an Indian archer, neither shield nor breastplate. They carry on their left arm targets of raw ox-hide, narrower than the men who carry them, but not much inferior in length. Others have javelins instead of arrows. All wear a sword broad and not less than three cubits in length." They had on their side no machine for throwing stones or darts, nor any very long spears or pointed pikes like the Macedonian *sarissa*, 24 feet in length. Their only hope of repelling the enemy with missiles lay on their large bows. But on that fateful day these proved unavailing, because these extremely weighty bows could not be strung nor discharged without resting one end of them on the ground, and the rain sodden Kari plain presented them with no hard surface for this purpose. Thus, while they were helplessly fumbling the bow-string, the enemy was upon them and cut them down. The English longbow archers had no such disadvantage on the damp field of Agincourt.

Even in defence, the Indian infantry was handicapped by inferiority of equipment. Unlike the Macedonians, they wore no armour, and thus had no metallic plate to protect their heads and breasts. Their shields were made of a coiled cane branch frame (Greek word *wicker-shield*), with a cover of raw ox-hide, but not metal-coated. Hence, in the battle of Platea, the Asiatic infantry taken by Xerxes to Greece, were butchered like sheep by the Greeks. "The wicker-shields of the Asiatic bowmen were no defence. At close quarters the Spartan hoplite's armour and Dorian spear soon decided the issue." (Cambridge Anc. His., iv 340).

Thus in the battle with Alexander, our infantry, like our chariot arm, was neutralised, except during the last stage of hand to hand fighting, when the larger reach of the Macedonian swords and spears robbed the Indians of every chance of returning blows with effect.

(iii) *Cavalry*:—The cavalry mounted on short country-born ponies, was the weakest arm of Poros's army. On the other hand, the horsemen of Alexander were superior not only in number but immeasurably so in efficiency, the height and strength of their horses (of the choice Arab and Kabul breeds), and the armour protection of both rider and mount. There were no mounted archers on the Indian side, to match the Scythian bowmen on horses serving Alexander for hire. The Indian cavalryman carried two darts, like what the Greeks called *saunia* (*i.e.*, not more than 9 feet long) and a shield smaller than that of the infantry. (Megasthenes quoted by Arrian, p. 419).

These facts decided the issue in the initial cavalry encounter, and prevented any attempt at rear-guard defence by the Indians after their defeat at the end of the day.

(iv) *Elephants*:—Each elephant carried three fighters and only one driver, so that the elephant became uncontrolled like a derelict ship when the *mahut* was shot off its back by long range missiles. (Tarn, i.96). On the other hand, each chariot carried a second driver as a reserve.

CHAPTER III

ALEXANDER'S BATTLE WITH POROS: STRATEGY AND TACTICS

Paurav (Greek spelling Poros) was the noblest of the Indian kings of his time. He ruled over the upper Jech Doab, or the land enclosed by the Jhelum river (Greek 'Hydaspes', from the Sanskrit *Vitasta*) on the west and the Chenab on the east. His greatest enemy was Ambhi (Greek Ohphi), the king of Taxila (near modern Hasan Abdal), and his ally was Abhisar, the king of Rajaur and Jamu. After overcoming the last two, Alexander called upon Poros to pay tribute and wait upon the Macedonian conquerer at his own frontier. By this envoy Poros sent back the reply that he would comply only with the second of these demands, and when Alexander entered his realm he would meet him but come armed for battle. (Q. Curtius).

Alexander, determined to crush his spirit of independence as an offence to himself, marched down to the west bank of the Jhelum and encamped at a place opposite Poros's camp on the other bank, about the middle of May, 326 B.C.

"The Macedonians had their native wives and children with them, and there were scientific men and experts, camp-followers and traders; with the auxiliary services, and the contingents supplied later by Indian princes, there may well have been (as tradition suggests) 1,20,000 souls in the camp on the Hydaspes. The army had become a moving State". (Professor Tarn).

The Jhelum at this point was a very swift stream, fully half a mile in breadth, and the approaching monsoon rain would soon make it impassable. On the eastern bank stood Poros's huge war elephants (85 are mentioned by the Greeks) near the water's edge, and behind them were massed his infantry and cavalry ready to oppose the landing of the Macedonians. As Alexander said, the uncouth shape of the elephants and their violent trumpeting and movement of the trunk would have frightened his horses into jumping from their boats into water. So, a crossing in the face of such a foe was not practicable.

Alexander pondered, surveyed the west bank up and down, and played a master stroke of strategy to steal a passage 17 miles upstream, unopposed by the enemy. For this purpose he halted there for five weeks and deluded the enemy by daily making false demonstrations of crossing the river there, with marching of troops and loud noises, but not actually embarking. So he at last succeeded in making Poros believe that the Macedonians did not mean business and meant to retire baffled. Thus the Indian army was thrown off its guard and slackened its vigilance.

Meantime, Alexander had chosen the place for his secret crossing at a spot 17 miles upstream from his camp, where a high bluff covered with trees on the west bank at a sharp bend in the river and a wooded island in midstream facing it, shortened the distance to be ferried over and fully concealed his movements from Poros's camp. Here long row-boats had been conveyed by being taken to pieces, transported inland on carts, joined together again, and kept concealed in the jungles for the day of need. Also numbers of skins had been collected which were to be stuffed with dry grass, stitched, and made to serve as floats or pontoons, on which planks were to be laid for ferrying the horses over.

One dark night Alexander started from his camp in secret with nearly three-fourths of his troops, the remaining forces being left behind in the camp under Krateros with orders to keep up Poros's delusion that Alexander was still there and also to detain a part of the Indian army to oppose his crossing after Poros had learnt that Alexander had actually come over to his side of the river and the Indian king would march out to give him battle.

By following a sunken road some distance parallel to the river bank, Alexander reached the appointed place without the enemy and most of the people in his own camp knowing of his march. Then he safely crossed over to the wooded island in midstream. Here a most violent thunderstorm with a deluge of rain burst upon his men and it was also discovered, to heighten their terror and perplexity, that the island did not touch the east bank, but the narrow and shallow channel on that side had been turned by the rush of water from the hills into another raging torrent, which had struck the east bank, flooding its low-lying beach and causing huge land slips by undercutting the high bank.

Nothing daunted, Alexander cheered his troops and made them cross this second channel also, himself leading in the first boat, and transporting the horses on the inflated skin rafts. On the east bank the landing was at last effected by wading through breast-high water where the night's rain had flooded the low beach and formed a bay. Only one boat was lost, by being dashed against a rock and sunk. All the others crossed in safety. By this time the sun had risen, the rain ceased, and the night gloom was dispersed. It was a symbolic reward of such an iron-willed leader of men and the tough soldiers who followed him.

Alexander's crossing of the Jhelum was a feat of strategic genius equalled only by Marlborough's piercing the Ne Plus Ultra lines in France, but it was carried out under far greater difficulties and even more faultlessly accomplished. If it be objected that Marlborough was matched against an equally civilised and well-equipped foe, while on the Jhelum Greeks fought barbarians, it must be remembered that Alexander was struck in the midst of his journey by such an unexpected fury of the elements as would have baffled any one except such a heaven-born general and his hard-bitten soldiers.

Forming his troops in order on the dry land, Alexander advanced with his cavalry towards Poros's camp down the bank, ordering his infantry to follow more slowly. Half the way had not been crossed when he sighted an Indian force coming up to reconnoitre. It was a corps of 1000 horses and 60 chariots, under a son of Poros. The young prince was hopelessly outnumbered, getting no time to form a line and adopt tactics of defence. Alexander attacked him with his cavalry charging by squadrons while his horse-archers turned the enemy's flanks. The prince was killed with 400 of his men, the rest fled away to carry the fatal news to Poros. "The chariots were captured, horses and all, for they proved heavy in the retreat and useless in action itself by having stuck fast in the clay". (Arrian.)

Poros was at first distracted, by one enemy force threatening to cross the river and fall on his camp from the west and the great conqueror himself coming down upon him with his main army by land from the north. But at last he decided to leave a few elephants and a small force in his camp to oppose the landing of Krateros, and himself marched with the remaining troops to meet Alexander on the way.

The encounter took place on the Kari plain. When Alexander leading his vanguard of cavalry sighted the army of Poros, he halted for some time beyond bowshot of the enemy, in order to allow his infantry to come up and recover their breath, while he himself rode along the Indian front to reconnoitre.

There stood Poros's troops drawn up in battle order on a dry sandy patch of the Kari plain, their left obliquely inclined towards the Jhelum and their position clear of the mud pools here and there on their right and rear. On their extreme left were the quicksands of Sukaytur.

In the front of the Indian line were stationed 85 elephants with fighters on their howdas (which the Greeks likened to castles), a hundred feet apart from one another, the spaces between them being filled by the best-equipped infantry (called men-at-arms by the Greeks). Behind this front line was massed other infantry, but the vast number of foot soldiers could not at all be crowded into the space behind the elephants,—two large bodies of infantry projected on the right and left wings, in line with their brethren in the centre but with their front unprotected by any elephants. These two wings were further extended right and left by the Indian cavalry, probably 3,000 strong in two equal divisions, which formed the extreme wings of the Indian army.

Poros had two hundred war-chariots still with him; these were posted in two equal divisions of a hundred each on his right and left, beyond the elephants, and in front of the infantry of the wings. The total strength of the Indian army was about 33,000 and of the Macedonian a little over 15,000 (Tarn). In the centre of the line of elephants, on the tallest elephant in the field could be seen the towering figure of Poros, nearly seven feet in height, "his armour embellished with gold and silver set off his supremely majestic person to great advantage. His courage matched his bodily vigour, and his wisdom was the utmost attainable in a rude community", as the polished Quintus Curtius Rufus acknowledges.

After reconnoitring the enemy's formation, Alexander quickly marshalled his own ranks. On his extreme right he concentrated all his cavalry, over five thousand strong, consisting of four complete regiments of the Macedonian horse (the best troops in his army) two of them under Koinos and two under himself and next to them on the left the thousand horse-archers serving as very flexible and useful light cavalry. His centre was formed by the infantry, first a corps of light infantry, next the Hypaspists (under Seleukos) and then five battalions of the phalanx (under Antigenes, Kleitus, Meleager, Attalus and Gorgias). Finally another corps of light infantry formed the extreme of his left wing,—which last, as can be easily seen, was made very much weaker than his right wing because it was this right wing and centre that he intended to do the real work for him.

The Indian army lay on the defensive a huge inert mass, wanting to observe their enemy's action. Alexander, on the other hand, seized the initiative, thus enjoying the advantage of attacking or drawing back at any point as suited his interest, and varying his tactics with every change in the tide of the battle. His plan was not to throw away his soldiers by hurling them against the hard core of the enemy's line, namely, the centre protected by the elephants and supported by the enemy's best infantry. So, he held the phalanx stationary before the Indian centre as a threat paralysing its movement to aid any wing, while he sought a decision by first attacking the Indian left wing. He would begin by tempting the Indian cavalry (1,500 on the left) to come out of its defensive position, and while it was thrown into temporary disorder by movement he would overwhelm it by superior numbers and tactics. It was only after this decision had been reached on the Indian left wing that the Macedonian centre (all infantry) should attack the men opposite to them. This was exactly the policy of Wellington who in his Maratha battles (as later in the Peninsula) made it a point never to attack the enemy when holding a defended position, but only when they were on the move and thrown into disorder by the broken ground.[1]

Combat Opens

When the fighting became general, the Indian chariots drove at full speed into the middle of the battle, to aid their friends. Some Macedonian foot soldiers, first exposed to this charge, were trampled down, while the charioteers were hurled from their seats, when the chariots in rushing into action jolted over broken and slippery ground. Some of the horses also took fright and precipitated the carriages not only into the sloughs and pools of water but even into the river itself. (Q. Curtius). So, this arm of the Indian army could achieve nothing useful and soon ceased to exist. In that clash of myriads of men, only 200 chariots could have done little service, even if they had not been bogged.

Centre Attacked

As soon as the Indian cavalry was driven off its post by Alexander and Koinos, the phalanx advanced (as previously ordered by Alexander) and attacked the line of elephants and the infantry men forming the centre. Then began the most stubborn and murderous part of the fight. The elephants were driven against the attacking infantry, and the onslaught of these huge uncouth monsters was a kind of warfare of which the Macedonian soldiers had no experience before. The elephants charged and "wherever they turned went crushing through the Macedonian phalanx though in close formation" (Arrian). Some of the enemy they lifted up with their trunks and hurled down to the ground or trampled under foot. The front line

---

[1] The Combat opened with Alexander sending his mounted archers (one thousand strong) to attack the Indian cavalry opposite (about 1,500) and throw them into confusion with a storm of arrows and charges of horses. Behind them he himself advanced with two full regiments (and the Royal Guard, 2,300), while he sent off two other cavalry regiments (2,000 men) under Koinos with order to ride round the back and left flank of his archers and attack the cavalry of the Indian left in the rear, while they were entangled with Alexander himself in front. As the battle opened the cavalry on the extreme right of the Indian army, rode away from their posts to succour their brethren on the left.

of the Macedonian army quailed, but it was for a moment only. Alexander's light troops and varying tactics enabled him to master this danger.

As Q. Curtius describes the scene,—"These animals inspired great terror, and their strange dissonant cries frightened not only the horses, which shy at everything, but the men also, and disordered the ranks, so that the victors began to look round for flight. Alexander thereupon despatched against the elephants the lightly armed Agrianians and the Thracian troops, more serviceable in skirmishing than in close combat. They assailed the elephants and their drivers with a furious storm of missiles, and the phalanx, on seeing the resulting terror and confusion, steadily pressed forward".

Seeing the first confusion of the phalanx in the struggle with the elephants, the Indian cavalry, so long sheltering behind their elephant line, wheeled round and charged Alexander's cavalry on their left. But the Macedonians, being "far superior in personal strength and military discipline (and I must add, the size and spirit of their horses), again routed them and drove them back upon the elephants." Alexander's genius was shown by his use of a mass of heavy cavalry acting in small tactical units, as the striking force. This had led to his victories over the Persian royal armies. The close co-operation between foot and horse, which was a characteristic of Macedonian battle tactics, had been learnt from the Theban general Epaminondas. "The originality of Epaminondas's tactics lay in this that he had discovered the master principle that the quickest and most economical way of winning a military decision is to defeat the enemy not at his weakest but at his strongest point". [C.A.H. VI. 358 and 82.]

The whole of Alexander's cavalry had now been gathered into one command and did great havoc among the Indians cooped up in their centre. The elephants too, being now huddled together within a narrow space trampled down friends and foes alike as they wheeled and pushed about. Many of the elephant drivers had been shot down, some of the elephants had been wounded, and being thus rendered frantic and without a guide the animals roamed over the field aimlessly, attacking all who lay in their path. Their victims now were mostly Indians, because, "the Macedonians, who had a wide and open field and could therefore operate as they thought best, gave way when the elephants charged, and when the beasts retreated followed at their heels and plied them with darts; whereas the Indians who were in the midst of the animals, suffered far more the effects of their rage". At last the utterly exhausted elephants retreated but still keeping their faces to the enemy "like ships backing water" and trumpeting. (Arrian).

The fight had raged for over three hours now, with increasing crowding and confusion on the Indian side. Central command and co-operation among their parts had vanished; everywhere a mingled fight was going on. In the Indian army, "The king's authority was unheeded, and the ranks being broken, as many took the command upon themselves as there were scattered bodies of troops. Every one began to dictate some tactics of his own". No common plan of action was after all concerted." (Q. Curtius).

Indians Routed

The Indian cavalry was mostly cut up. But the heaviest slaughter was among our infantry. They were hopelessly butchered, as their enormous bows could not be strung by resting one end on the soft ground, and the Macedonian spears were much longer than the Indian swords. At the closing stage of the struggle, Poros gathered his remaining friends together and rallying his forces near about advanced with some elephants to prolong the contest. The battle continued doubtful for some time longer, the Macedonians sometimes pursuing, and sometimes fleeing from the elephants.

At last, while the blood of the Indian army was ebbing away and the elephants were worked off their feet or wounded, the end came. At the right moment Alexander surrounded with his cavalry the whole of the enemy's line and gave the signal that his infantry with their shields linked together so as to give the utmost compactness to their ranks, should advance in a solid column. The Macedonians were now pressing upon the remnant of Poros's army from every side. All turned to flight, wherever they could find a gap in the cordon of Macedonian cavalry (Arrian). It was the eighth hour of the day.

Poros had maintained the contest so long as he had a single follower left. Two of his sons and most of his gallant friends (one of whom was named Pitak or Spittak) had fallen by this time. As the enemy came up to him, he began to hurl upon them the spears of which he had kept a supply on his elephant, but he himself was exposed as a conspicuous target to the arrows and darts of enemy. He had received nine wounds before and behind, the worst of which was in his right shoulder where he was unprotected by armour. "Faint from the great loss of blood, his hands dropped the darts rather than hurled them. At last he turned his elephant's head and began to retire, soon afterwards falling down senseless in his howda. According to one account, his sagacious elephant retired of itself when its master collapsed on its back.

In this time Krateros had arrived across the river with the full battalions of the phalanx (3,000 strong) from Alexander's camp, and he now took up the pursuit with these fresh troops. It was Blucher arriving after Waterloo had been fought and won by Wellington; and the pursuit was carried on with vigour. Alexander had issued orders that no quarter was to be given to the enemy, but all were to be killed, resisting or unarmed and surrendering themselves as captives.

Poros himself was taken prisoner and made a friend by Alexander's generous policy. The loss on the Indian side is exaggerated by Arrian to 23,000 men, while the Macedonian loss is minimised to 80 infantry and 230 horsemen. Diodoros gives a more sober estimate, 280 cavalry and more than 700 infantry slain on Alexander's side, and in the Indian army upwards of 12,000 men killed and 9,000 taken prisoner. This last figure proves how effective and relentless was the pursuit of an exhausted leaderless army by the fresh troops of Krateros. As Professor Tarn admits, "Alexander's losses were carefully concealed (in his despatches), but there is conclusive proof of the desperate nature of the battle with the elephants and its effect on the minds of the generals, specially on that of Seleukos."

Plutarch, the best ancient biographer of Alexander, confirms this view and adds, "The combat with Poros abated the spirit of the Macedonians, and made them resolve to proceed no further in India."

CHAPTER IV

ISLAMIC INVASIONS

Muslim Conquest

The Turkish invasions of India from Mahmud of Ghazni onwards have followed this uniform pattern and the result has always been the same,—India's final weakness against smaller but superiorly accoutred, mounted and led bodies of invaders. Before the blazing sun of the Indian summer can come to our aid, the invading horsemen from the cold northwestern hills have had five clear months (October to February) to do their work; they have overthrown the Hindu monarchies on the frontier, sacked cities (seldom stopping to besiege forts on hills), struck terror among the population, and retired to their mountain homes, enriched with plunder and the cession of some Indian district on the western frontier where they at first planted some local prince as a tribute-paying vassal.

The course of Turkish advance into India is plainly visible in our history. Before the Eastward Push of Islam began, the Kabul valley beyond the Khyber Pass was the kingdom of a Buddhist dynasty, probably Scythian, called Turki Shahi, which was followed by a Hindu Shahi line of kings. These latter were overthrown by an Arab family professing Islam, and their descendants were pushed beyond the Indus to Und (or Wahind, north of Attock). As yet Ghazni was a Buddhist district; but a Turki General of the Kabul Sultan made it a Muslim State, while the unconverted remnant of the Buddhist population took refuge in the obscure region on the shore of the Ab-i-Istada lake, and it was some centuries before they were Islamized.

The Ghazni ruler gained Kabul. And from Kabul as a base, the Turkish horsemen with some Afghan followers attracted by the hope of plunder, invaded the Hindu province next to its eastern frontier and plundered and weakened it as the result of the first year's compaigning. The defeated Hindu Raja made peace by promising to pay tribute and to recognise the Ghazni Sultan as his overlord. Next autumn the raid was repeated and further penetration into Hindu India effected. If the previously humbled Raja of the frontier district defaulted in paying his tribute,—which, was quite likely in his impoverished finances, or if he showed any manly spirit, he was destroyed in the second year's invasion and that province was annexed and placed under a Muslim Viceroy. Thus arose the first centre of Muslim power in India, and from it went forth year after year every autumn at first raiding and ultimately conquering parties to the Hindu Kingdom next on its eastern frontier, which in the course of two or three years suffered the same fate. Lured by reports of the fabulous wealth to be gained by plundering the Hindus, thousands of trans-frontier Turks and Pathans flocked to the conquering Sultan's banners every autumn, asking for no pay but only permission to plunder in his train. Thus the base of Muslim power in India was generation after generation shifted south-eastwards by the same process of raid, feudatory subordination, and full annexation, till the Muslim advance dashed against the hills of Assam.

If in any year the invaders from the north-west were unexpectedly held up by the Hindu defence, they could easily call up reinforcements from their own State just across the border, or retire baffled to come back next autumn in renewed strength to make victory sure. Their line of communication with Central Asia, the breeding ground of their soldiers and horses,—was kept unbroken behind them. But the opposite was the lot of the small Hindu States, disunited by love of local independence and the practice of their ruling Rajas not to tolerate a Hindu overlord, and torn by the jealous feud of clan against clan, caste against caste. Hindu religious philosophy may be sublime, but it does not teach the perfect social solidarity and equality of the faithful which is the noblest gift of Islam.

Turks and Their Wars

The enemy tribes that broke into India from the north-west were mounted archers and spearmen—at first Scythians such as Sakas, Huns and Parthians, and from 1000 A.D. onwards Muslims known by the race-name of Turks. These invaders were accompanied by bands of Afghans as their servants, who formed a second line and were converted to Islam a century or two later than the Turks.

Islam gave to its followers (as H. A. L. Fisher has pointed out) three characteristic virtues which no other religion has inspired so successfully, and which imparted to natural soldiers like the Arabs, Berbers, Pathans and Turks, a wonderful military efficiency. These were: *First*, complete equality and social solidarity, as regards legal status and religious privileges. Thus all distinctions of caste and race were swept away and the sect was knit together like the members of one vast family of brothers. *Secondly*, fatalism, springing from an absolute reliance on God and the belief that what Allah wills must triumph over every human effort. This bred contempt of death in fighting. *Thirdly*, freedom from drunkenness. Wine drinking is a sin according to the *Quran* and a crime punishable by the State in Muslim countries. On the other hand, wine drinking was the ruin of the Rajputs, Marathas, and other Hindu soldiers, and made them incapable of far-sighted military planning, conducting surprises, and even guarding their own camps with proper precaution.

The arms and horses of these trans-border invaders gave them indisputable military superiority over the Indians. Their provisions, also, were carried by fast-trotting camels, which required no fodder for themselves but fed on the roots and leaves on the wayside, while the Banjara pack-oxen of the Hindu commissariat were slow and burdensome.

The *Cambridge Medieval History*, Vol. I, p. 331, tells us—

"The Turkoman horse is the noblest in the whole of Central Asia, and surpasses all other breeds in speed, endurance, intelligence, faithfulness and a marvellous sense of locality. The Turkoman horse is tall, with a long narrow body, long thin legs and neck.... On their predatory expeditions the Turkomans often cover 650 miles in the waterless desert in five days.... They owe their powers to the training of thousands of years in the endless steppes and deserts, and to the continual plundering raids, which demanded the utmost endurance and privation of which horse and rider were capable."

The same thing was noticed by Shah Jahan's generals who invaded Balkh and fought the Uzbaks and Alamans (Turkoman tribes). They have written,—"These ferocious robbers were not hampered in their marches by any baggage or provisions; the coarsest food sufficed for them. The deepest rivers they crossed by swimming their horses in a long line, the bridle of one being fastened to the tail of another, while the saddles, which were mere bundles of sticks, could not be damaged by water. The men crossed on rafts made from the reeds that grew plentifully on the river-bank. The horses, as hardy as their riders, lived on the wild worm-wood (*darmana*) of the steppe and yet could cover forty to fifty *kos* a day on this fodder!" (Abdul Hamid's *Padishahnamah*, Vol. II, p. 619.)

These were the Turkomans. Their southern neighbours, the Turks, were more civilised and a little,—but only a little, less hardy than they, but prized the Turkoman horses for their marching, besides purchasing Arab thoroughbreds. The Turks were so famous for the speed and vigour of their cavalry charges that in the Asiatic world the phrase *Turk-sawar* (i.e. Turkish horseman) became a general name for the richly accoutred superbly mounted dashing cavalry of any race. Even the 19th Dragoons of the English Army in India in 1802 are called in the Marathi and Persian records *Turk-sawars*, while the common Indian mounted troops are designated as mere *fauj*.

Now, for the weapons of the invaders. The composite bow (of two pieces joined together by a metal band) used by "the Iranian and Turkish nomads.... was the most dreaded weapon of antiquity," according to the *Cambridge Ancient History* (Vol. XII, p. 216). And such Oriental archers were enlisted in the army of the Roman Empire in the third century A.D.

"The Persian, Scythian, and Parthian bow was far more efficient than the Cretan (whose range was only 80 to 100 paces), while a javelin could pierce at 30 to 40 paces. The horse-archers in the Roman army (fourth century) discharged arrows "which pierced cuirass and shield with ease, and they shot equally well dismounted and at the gallop."

(*Encyclo. Brit.* 11th ed. ii. 363). What had the Hindu army to oppose to these weapons.

Mounted archers were employed as light troops for harassing and bewildering the enemy. But the Turkish nobles themselves fought as heavy cavalry,—clad in armour for both man and horse, and wielding long spears. Their massed charge was irresistible on the plains of north India.

The tactics of our Turkish invaders had been first developed by the ancient Persian empire before its decline and defeat at the hands of Alexander. This "mode of warfare consisted in disordering the enemy by archery fire and then charging him with cavalry"—i.e., the armoured heavy cavalry in which the Persians excelled. (*Cam. Anc. Hist.*, Vol. VI, 360.)

A typical Turkish battle—of the western Turks and not of India's invaders, the eastern Turks, was that of Manzikert (fought in 1071 in farther Armenia) which is thus graphically described by Gibbon (Chap. 57):—

"The Turkish Sultan Alp Arslan's hopes of victory were placed in the arrows of the Turkish cavalry, whose squadrons were loosely distributed in the form of a crescent. Instead of the successive lines and reserves of the Greek tactics,—the Eastern Roman Emperor Romanus led his army in a single and solid phalanx, and pressed with vigour and impatience the artful and yielding resistance of the barbarians. In this desultory and fruitless combat he wasted the greater part of a summer's day, . . . but no sooner had the standard been turned to the rear than the phalanx was broken. . . . The Turkish squadrons poured a cloud of arrows on this moment of confusion and lassitude; and the horns of the formidable crescent were closed in the rear of the Greeks."

This, with a few necessary changes, was exactly the tactics by which Prithvi-raj was defeated in 1192 at the second battle of Tarain.

Oman describes the above battle very clearly thus:—

The Seljuck army "was a great horde of horse-archers . . . more than a hundred thousand strong. . . . The Turks, after their usual manner, made no attempt to close or to deliver a general attack on the Imperial host. Large bodies of horse-archers hovered about and plied their bows against various points of the line. . . . (At last in the evening) the Turks began to steal round the wings and to molest the fighting line from behind.... The right wing in trying to face both ways, fell into disorder in the twilight, and at last broke up and fled. The victors at once fell on the flank and rear of the centre... and the Turks broke into the column and made a dreadful slaughter... the whole centre was cut to pieces. Thus (the Roman Emperor) paid the penalty for attacking a swarm of horse-archers in open rolling country, where he had cover neither for his flanks nor for his rear." *Art of War in M. Ages* (1st ed.) 217-219.

The eastward push of Islamic arms into India can be exactly traced in history. It followed one uniform pattern; at first for some years raids across the frontier, in the next stage invasions in force leading to pitched battles in which the nearest Hindu king was defeated and humbled into a vassal and his kingdom made a friendly base for further advance into Hindustan, and finally the vassal, after one last futile struggle, was extinguished and his kingdom annexed to the Muslim empire. Thus, our border provinces were nibbled away year by year, and the Islamic dominion pushed deeper and deeper into the North Indian plains. This process continued for centuries, till the foreign flood was arrested and driven back by the wild hills, jungles and earthquakes of Assam and the untamed valour of the Ahom race in the 17th century.

When this eastward sweep of Islam began, Afghanistan and all North India were under the rule of Hindu kings. The Turki Shahi Hindu kings of Kabul lost that city and north-west Afghanistan to the Sultans of the Samana dynasty early in the 10th century. A Turki slave of this dynasty named Alp-Tigin founded an independent kingdom of his own at Ghazni (reign, 950-963). His son Sabuk-Tigin (r. 963-997) attacked Jaipal I, the Hindu king of Eastern Afghanistan, whose capital had been shifted to Ohind (Und), 15 miles north of Attock, where the Indus was easier to cross, because that place was above its junction with the Kabul river. In 990 Amir Sabuk-Tigin defeated Jaipal and compelled him to cede Jallalabad (Laghman district, in Eastern Afghanistan) and he thus approached the Khyber Pass. In 991, after defeating Jaipal again, near Kuram, the Amir took Peshawar and thus made a lodgement east of the Khyber Pass within easy striking distance of the Panjab plains, which were now separated from him by the Indus river only. In an attempt to recover Peshawar, Jaipal was defeated (27th November, 1001). Stung by the shame of his successive defeats, the Hindu king abdicated and committed suicide (1002). His son Anandpal was defeated by Sabuk-Tigin's successor, the famous conqueror Mahmud of Ghazni (reign 997-1030).

In 1004 Mahmud made himself master of Multan and Uch (west of Bahawalpur) and just below the junction of the Indus with the other four rivers of the Panjab. In 1005 Mahmud defeated Anandpal again and placed the old capital Und under a vassal of his own. With the Turks sitting astride the Indus, and holding a line of crossing places on it, the natural geographical defence of India was broken and the Muslim penetration of Hindustan became an easy thing. On 31st December, 1008, Mahmud crushed the forces of Anandpal somewhere between Und and Peshawar. The Hindu king had shifted his capital to Nandana. His successor, named Jaipal II, was defeated here and his capital placed under a vassal of the Ghazni Sultan. The permanent result of the many expeditions of Mahmud into India was the formation of North Panjab into a transmontane province of the Ghazni kingdom with Lahore for its governor's seat. In this city Mahmud's weak descendants took refuge when they lost their Afghan territories to the house of Ghor. It was these Sultans of Ghor who established the first Muslim empire in India. In 1186 Shihabuddin Ghori (also known as Muizuddin Muhammad bin Sam) forced Khusrau Malik, the last crowned descendant of the mighty Mahmud of Ghazni, to surrender Lahore to him, only to be extinguished in prison.

With a Muslim dynasty planted at Lahore and able to draw hardy reinforcements from its dominions in Afghanistan, the safety of the plains of Hindustan was lost. Though no systematic invasion or raid in force was attemped during the 160 years from the death of Mahmud of Ghazni to the first invasion of Shihabuddin Ghori, individual Turkish adventurers used frequently to try their luck by raids into Delhi and other Hindu provinces further east. One expedition in great force was carried out by Tugha-Tigin, the chief minister of Masaud III (reign, 1099-1115) of Ghazni. This general "crossed the Ganges in order to carry on a holy war against Hindustan and penetrated to a place where except Sultan Mahmud no one had reached so far with an army before." (*Tabaqat-i-Nasiri*, i. 107). This language clearly implies many other but lesser raids from Lahore.

The disruption of government and the terror caused by these frequent Turkish forays are also proved by the levy of a tax on land called *Turushka-danda*, by the local Rajas of North India, for paying an annual blackmail to the Muslims beyond the frontier. (See the copper plate inscriptions of the Gaharwar kings of Kanauj.) Its nature was the same as that of Dane-geld in Anglo-Saxon England, collected for paying to the Scandinavian pirates who used to infest the country.

Chapter V

SHIHABUDDIN GHORI VS. PRITHVIRAJ

By the time that the Ghori Sultan began his invasion of Hindusthan, a great change had taken place in the social organisation of this country. We now find a peculiar race, called *Rajputs* (i.e., sons of Rajas) and Kshatriyas by caste, holding the rulers' place all over the country from the Satlej to the Son river. Near the close of the 12th century, their clans were thus distributed:—

The Chauhan Raja of Sambhar, with Ajmer as his chief town, had recently conquered Delhi (formerly held by a Tomar chief) and formed a large kingdom which stood as the first western barrier to the advance of the Turks. East of him lay the large kingdom of Kanauj under a Raja of the Gaharwar clan (later to be called Rathor) and embracing all the country south-eastwards up to Benares. South of the centre lay the lands of the Chandel clan in what came later to be called Bundelkhand, with their chief forts Mahoba and Kalinjar. But within this area there were constant feuds between clan and clan, king and king, and the Hindu Powers could offer no united opposition to the foreign invaders, except on a few rare occasions, and even then their confederated forces were too ill-knit and too slowly mobilised to win decisive success.

The gallant Prithviraj Chauhan, lord of Ajmer and Delhi, had fought a long war with Paramardi, the Chandel Raja, and captured his city of Mahoba. Later, he had mortally offended Jaychand, the Raja of Kanauj by defeating his ambition to declare himself Paramount Sovereign by the ceremony of Horse-sacrifice, (*ashwa-medh*) and carrying off his daughter at a "Bride's choice" (*Swayamban*). But most Rajas of North India flocked to his side when he first stood up to oppose the Muslim invaders. The bone of contention between the two Powers was the fort of Bhatinda, 100 miles south of Lahore and 180 miles north-west of Delhi, which had once been the last capital of the Hindu kings of North Panjab and now stood as the border fortress of the kingdom of Ajmer-Delhi. Shihabuddin Ghori took it in 1190, left a garrison of 1,200 horses in it under Qazi Zia-ud-din, and set out on his return home. But he was soon called back from the way by the news that Prithviraj at the head of a vast allied force was advancing to recover it. Shihabuddin, without waiting for reinforcements turned back at once with what forces he had with himself to anticipate the enemy and rapidly advanced to Taraori, 125 miles south-east of Bhatinda and twelve miles south of Thaneswar.[1]

The first great battle for the lordship of Hindustan followed. The Hindus greatly outnumbered the Turks, and this superiority enabled them to overlap their enemy's line of battle on the two flanks. The battle joined as the Hindus gave the signal for attack by blowing conchshells from the backs of elephants, while the Muslims struck their kettledrums carried on camels and sounded their trumpets. The impetuous charge of the Rajputs scattered like a cloud the Muslim vanguard, composed of "Afghan and Khokar braggarts".

Advancing further, they turned both wings of the Turkish army and inclining inwards dispersed their opponents and threatened the centre, where the Sultan commanded in person. Large numbers of his horsemen began to slip away, not daring to face the roaring tide of Rajput cavalry flushed with victory. The Sultan was urged to save himself by flight as he had no supporter left. But scorning such cowardly counsel, he made a reckless charge into the body of Rajputs before him, hewing his way with his sword, and followed by a small body of devoted companions. Govind Rai (the Governor of Delhi), who led the vanguard of his brother Prithviraj, on sighting Shihabuddin

[1] Prithviraj "defeated Md. Bin Sam Ghori at *Naraina*, seven miles from Karnal and three from Taraori. This village is situated on the Nai Nadi. Next year the Sultan returned and defeated and killed Prithviraj on the same spot." "*Tiraori* (*sic*). Here Azam Shah, son of Aurangzib, was born. In memory of him the place was named Azimabad. A wall round the town, a mosque, and a tank, said to have been built by Aurangzib are still in existence. The old highway ran through Tiraori, and there is a well preserved old royal *sarai* here. ("*Karnal Dist. Gazetteer*, 1884, pp. 27 *and* 264). *Taraori* is a railway station 9 miles north of Karnal city and 12 miles south of Thaneswar station. Nai Nadi flows in two branches close on the west of the walled village of Taraori. *Indian Atlas*, Sheet-18 S.W.

from a distance, drove his elephant towards him. The two leaders met in single combat. The Sultan's lance knocked out two of Govind Rai's front teeth, while the Hindu Chief hurled a javelin which inflicted a severe wound on the upper arm of Shihabuddin and forced him to turn his horse's head round in agony and weakness. However, he was saved from falling down, by a Khalj youth who leaped upon his horse from behind, kept him on the saddle with his arms, and urging the horse on by word of mouth, carried him away to the base in safety. The rout of the Turki army was complete, but such a victory did not yield its full fruits as the Rajputs were incapable of making a relentless pursuit, and their ponies were outpaced by the Khurasani horses of the Muslim army. Prithviraj merely followed up his victory by laying siege to Bhatinda, which held out for thirteen months and at last capitulated. (probable date September 1192).

Sultan Shihabuddin set himself to avenge this defeat. Arrived at home he publicly disgraced and cashiered all his captains who had shown such cowardice at Taraori. In a year and a half he raised for the next Indian expedition a vast force of Turki and Afghan military adventurers, estimated by an eye-witness at "120,000 cavalry clad in armour" (*Tabaqat-i-Nasiri*, i. 465). When he reached Peshawar he had the wisdom of pardoning his lately dismissed captains and summoning them to his side for a chance of wiping out their disgrace. They gladly joined him with their contingents. The day after their arrival, with his strength now raised to his utmost, he began his march towards Delhi.

The Hindu army this time was much smaller than in the first battle. Prithviraj had delayed in mobilising his force; many of his former allies were too lazy or indifferent to fight again for him, and his domestic enemy, the Raja of Kanauj, held off in unpatriotic pride. With what forces could be readily collected Prithviraj took his stand near the old battle-field of Taraori on the bank of the Saraswati.

Shihabuddin, avoiding Bhatinda, now in enemy hands, on his way, arrived some ten miles in front of the Hindu army. Here he received a friendly warning from Prithviraj, asking him to save his soldiers' lives by going back without fighting, as the

Hindu army, whose valour he had tested before, was large and was daily receiving reinforcements; at the same time the Raja swore by his gods that he would allow a safe passage to the Turki army without attacking it during the disorder of retreat.

Shihabuddin, "following the Prophet's words that war is a kind of deception (*al harb khada*)", played a cunning trick. He replied, "It is very generous and friendly of you to make this offer of peace. I am sending a messenger to my brother, who is the reigning Sultan, urging him to agree to make peace with you on the condition of Bhatinda, the Panjab and Multan remaining with the House of Ghor and the rest of Hindusthan under the Rajas. Pending the arrival of his reply, I beg you to suspend hostilities". (Firishtah).

The *ruse* proved a complete success. The simple trustful Rajputs swallowed the bait, and believing the invader's pacific tone to be due to his fear of their valour and a sense of his own weakness in numbers, they made no preparation for action and even neglected the common alertness necessary in the face of an enemy. Shihabuddin, on his part, lost no time. He matured his plan for attacking the Hindus the very next morning, because, while his army was now at its fullest strength, every day's delay meant some addition to his enemy's ranks and the consumption of his own provisions in idleness. He, therefore, set his army in motion some hours before day-break, covered the intervening miles unmolested and secured a lodgement in front of the Hindu camp before they could take the alarm.

It was the early dawn of a winter's day. The deluded Hindus were totally off their guard. Most of their soldiers had come out of their quarters into the waste land around for answering the call of nature or taking their morning bath. But so vast and sprawling was the Hindu camp that the surprise caused no disaster to it, especially as Shihabuddin held his men in hand instead of dispersing them by dashing attacks. The aggressor, however, gained two great advantages;

(1) He seized the tactical initiative and forced the Hindus to fight on the ground and in the manner of the Turk's own choosing, instead of the defenders delivering any attack planned

and prepared for before. In fact, all day long the Rajputs had to dance exactly as Shihabuddin played the tune.

(2) The Hindus had to fight on empty stomachs.

This last needs explanation today. It was the Hindu practice to prepare for a pitched battle by waking at 3 o'clock in the morning, performing the morning wash and worship, eating the cooked food (*pakwan*) kept ready beforehand, putting on arms, and marching out to their appointed places in the line of battle at sunrise. (See Mahadji Sindhia's preparations before setting out for the battle of Tunga or Lalsot, 1787). But in the second battle of Taraori, the Rajputs could take no breakfast; they had to snatch up their arms and form their lines as best as they could in a hurry.

Shihabuddin's plan of battle was to give the Rajput cavalry no chance for their shock tactics which had proved irresistible in his first encounter with them, but to make them move as he willed. He had left his heavy baggage, stores, elephants and non-combatants in his camp, ten miles behind, and advanced in light kit with his fighters only. His cavalry, all archers, were placed in four divisions of about 10,000 men each, who formed his vanguard, right and left wings, and rear (by which last term I understand the advanced reserve, called *iltmish* in the Turki language, whose duty it was to support the van or any wing from behind, when hard pressed). They were ordered to advance turn by turn and keep the Rajputs in play by shooting at them from a distance, but when the Indians advanced to engage them they were to feign flight and retreat beyond a horse's course, so as not to be entangled in combat. The real striking force of Shihabuddin was a corps of 12,000 steel-clad warriors, select men mounted on superb horses, kept under his personal command, as "strength in reserve," in the centre, a short distance behind the front line of attack. They were to be launched at the right moment to decide the issue.

These Parthian tactics bewildered and baffled the Hindus. They spent all their energy and time in the futile game of chasing and trying to catch up the elusive Central Asian horsemen before them. In this fashion the battle, or rather the series of skirmishes, raged from 9 o'clock in the morning till 3 o'clock in the afternoon, at the end of which the Hindus were utterly disspirited by the futility of their exertions and exhausted from hunger and thirst. Their rigid caste rules prevented them from being readily refreshed with food and drink in the battle front.

After such an unconquerable lassitude had seized the Hindu ranks, Shihabuddin gave the signal. His 12,000 choice heavy cavalry advanced like a solid wedge smashing their way through the loose-knit wavering Rajput ranks. Nothing could stand before such shock tactics. In a twinkle of the eye the battle was over. The Hindus broke into a hopeless flight in which tens of thousands of them were cut down unresisting. Govind Rai, the leader of the van had been killed earlier, and now Prithviraj himself, who had changed his elephant for a horse, was swept away by the tide of fugitives, captured on the bank of the Saraswati, and put to death in cold blood, to appease Shihabuddin's wrath. With him fell many others of the 150 Hindu Rajas who had joined the national confederacy. Legend and song have preserved the names of only some of these martyrs of liberty, such as Malesi, the Kachhwa chief.

Chapter VI

MILITARY ORGANISATION OF TURKS

Timur's Invasion 1398

During a period of three centuries and a half from 1192 to 1526, the first Turki empire of North India passed through a course of conquest, advance and consolidation under its early rulers, but gradually it lost its vital energy and lapsed into stagnation and dissolution, at last yielding the throne to an Afghan immigrant clan. This period differs in three respects from the next epoch in our history, which is called the Mughal Empire:

First, the political connection between Delhi and Afghanistan was lost, and recruits could no longer be regularly drawn from that country across the frontier passes by the Indian Government.

Secondly, baronial rebellion weakened the central Government, except under a few strong rulers.

Thirdly, fire-arms were unknown in war.

Then for 212 years, from 1526 to 1738, North India enjoyed a stable centralised Government, which spread over a part of the Deccan also, and kept the feudal vassals under control. It used fire-arms in war and began to import European arts, technique and teachers, and held Afghanistan under its sway. But in 1738 Nadir Shah's invasion shook this political fabric to pieces, detached Afghanistan once more from India, and by encouraging the Maratha inroads and the Sikh upheaval, prepared the way for the downfall of the native sovereignty and the establishment of British domination.

Zengis Khan's Army

The Mughal empire of Delhi was founded by Zahiruddin Babur, sixth in the line of descent from Timur, and he inherited the tradition of Timur. To understand Babur's army and tactics we must study those of Timur, and to understand Timur's military power aright we must go back to the war-machine of Zengis Khan (Chingis), who was Babur's ancestor in the female line. Each improved upon the organisation and technique of his predecessor, with certain necessary modifications. For instance, Timur had much more civilised tools than Zengis, and Babur had a very much smaller army and territorial resources than Timur, which were compensated for by his possession of a novel instrument of wonderful efficiency, namely fire-arms, unknown to his opponents. Zengis Khan (1154-1227 A.D.), showed his genius by uniting under one banner countless hordes of savage nomads,—Tartars (also called Mongols), Turks and other Scythian races. He imposed iron discipline over this miscellaneous multitude,—totalling seven lakhs of armed men, according to the chroniclers. His success was due to his strict organisation, unfailing choice of able lieutenants, and his wise policy of allowing complete religious toleration to every creed in his camp. No other general in history has shown such power of making so many diverse tribes and sects unite in forming one compact military machine.

His military organisation was based on five principles:—First, the regular division of troops into compact bands of regiments (Turki word *Kushun*, nominally one thousand), and brigades (Turki word *Tuman*, nominally ten thousand), each under a head and duly graded. Secondly, the enforcement of strict discipline by constant inspection and ruthless punishment of offenders. Thirdly, unfailing selection of able lieutenants, each of whom could independently command a distant detachment, while co-ordinating with the general plan of the campaign. Fourthly, the creation of a *corps d'elite* of the royal guards, as the most efficient striking force. And, fifthly, the development of speed of movement, which was almost incredible in the case of such vast numbers in that age of barbarism.

"In the utterances ascribed to him, Chingis only emphasised his services to the establishment of order and discipline among his people and in the army... Under Chingis Khan order was created everywhere and to each (man, woman and child) his position was allotted—thus replacing the disobedience prevailing everywhere before his time." (W. Barthold in *En-*

cyclop. Islam, ii, 858). "Each officer and soldier was made responsible, under pain of death, for the safety and honour of his companions." (Gibbon, Ch. 64). "Of special importance for the military success of the Mongols was the creation of a numerous bodyguard (whose number reached 10,000, in 1206), with well-defined rules of their conduct in the Khan's camp. Discipline was maintained with the greatest strictness. A valuable means of maintaining discipline and of training and testing the soldiers, was the hunting expeditions organised on a great scale, in which all the prescriptions of military discipline were observed with the same exactness as in actual warfare." "Chingis, when Emperor, was able to surround himself with a narrower circle of men from among his vassals, on whom he could rely as upon himself." (W. Barthold.) Zengis Khan thus conquered the eastern world from the Adriatic to the Yellow Sea and planted Tartar rule over Russia for two centuries.

Timur's Organisation

Timur, who rose to be Asia's world-conqueror two centuries after Zengis Khan, belonged to a more civilised age and a more stable political system than those of his Tartar predecessor. He was the chief of the Chaghtai or eastern branch of the Turks, while the Sultans of Constantinople belonged to the Osmanli or western branch of the same race. Zengis was illiterate and most of his tribesmen had not yet shed their ancestral religion of paganism or spirit-worship. Timur and his Turks were Muslim converts with fiery zeal for propagating their new faith by the massacre and plunder of infidels. Islam enabled him to form intimate contacts with the rest of the Muhammadan world and thus strengthen himself easily with the services of the learned men of Persia, Arabia and Egypt, as brethren of the faith. Nor was he a mere soldier; "he organised the administration and the army on rational basis"—and this ensured his unfailing success in a civilized world. (L. Bouvat in *Encyclop. Islam*. iv. 779).

By the time of Timur's invasion of Delhi (1398), the early Muslim conquerors of India had reached a sad state of decline. Two centuries of life in the ease and plenty of the soft climate of India had sapped their desert vigour and hardiness. The Delhi kingdom had not yet hardened into a strong and compact State, owing to the frequent disloyalty of the feudal barons and the civil wars caused by disputed succession, while their ill-subdued Hindu subjects were constantly rising in local rebellions which, though suppressed in the end, acted as an eternal drain on the resources of the Government. These early Turks and Afghans held India like an army of occupation; there was as yet no Indian nation, and no national defence was possible.

Timur had a first-rate military genius. He was also fortunate in gathering round himself a band of lieutenants of the highest capacity, each of whom he could safely trust with branch operations beyond his personal guidance. None of his opponents enjoyed this advantage. This conqueror's ruthless massacres of defeated enemies and surrendering civil populations, and authorised atrocities on the helpless people in his path, created a terror which cowed all thought of opposition to him. Utter desolation spread wherever his arms could reach, and even in advance of his path.

Timur's horsemen could ride 150 miles in one day and night, and march an average of 80 miles daily for a week together. This speed made their tactical dispersion and concentration for action an easy problem for their general, while it disconcerted all the defence plans of their enemies. Rivers,—except the raging floods during the Indian monsoon months, July to September,—formed no obstacle to these Turks. They swam their horses across them in a string, the tail of one horse being joined by a string to the head of the animal just behind it as they breasted the stream. Where necessary, Timur also built bridges of wood or of boats over the larger Indian rivers.

No doubt, his numbers alone,—92 squadrons of a thousand armour-clad cavalry each, would have overwhelmed his Indian opponents in the end. But Timur's strategy gave him immediate victory. His policy was always to seize the initiative. His incredibly swift movements and sharp decisive blows paralysed his enemies and confounded all their plans of battle and evacuation alike.

Timur Advances

Timur's invasion of Hindustan occupied only five months' time. After crossing the Indus on 24th September 1398, he proceeded south along the Jhilam river till near Jhang-i-Maghiana he crossed (10th October) the union of these two streams and entered the Rechna Doab. Pushing on further south he entered the Bari Doab after crossing the Ravi near Talamba (55 miles south of Jhang and 50 miles north-east of Multan) on 13th October. This town submitted but was sacked and the people massacred. On the 19th the march was resumed towards Multan.

Earlier in the year, his grandson Pir Muhammad (the son of Prince Jahangir) had been detached against the strong fortress of Multan. The prince first captured Uch (60 miles south of Multan) and then laid siege to Multan, which defied him for six months. At last this fort also fell, but the Indian monsoon bursting soon afterwards caused greater loss of men and horses to the detachment, and it was the 26th of October before the victorious prince could join his grandfather.

Next day the whole army began to cross over to the east bank of the Bias.[1] On 1st November 1398, Timur resumed his advance. One division of his army went towards Delhi by the Dipalpur route with orders to halt at Samana till joined by him. The second division, ten thousand select horsemen under Timur himself, pushed on towards Samana, by way of Pak Pattan, Khalis Kotali, Bhatner (which was stormed on 12th November after an 80-mile forced march in one day and night), Firuzabad fort, Sirsa, Fathabad, Tohana (18th November), to the bridge of Kohtila on the Ghagar river. Here the left detachment joined Timur. The heavy baggage and women were lodged in Samana, and

[1] The Bias at that time flowed 25 miles north-west of its present bed, and the Ravi ten miles south of its modern channel, in the longitude of Talamba. Timur's movements were Talamba to Jal (on the Bias, opposite Shahpur)—crosses the Bias to Janjan (?), 8 miles from Multan-Sahwal-Aswan-Jahwah-Dipalpur. The nearest approach to the word Janjan which I find in the survey map is Jakhar, 80 miles north-east of Multan and 25 miles n.e. of Talamba, while Shahpur is midway between Talamba and Jakhar. Harappa of prehistoric ruins is only 12 m. due east of Jakhar.

the combined fighting force reached Panipat on 4th December.[1]

Four days later (8th December) his advance guards reached the hillock on which stood Firuz Tughlaq's palace of *Jahan-numa*, later known as *Pahari*, less than half a mile west of the Lahore Gate of Shah Jahan's city. The Jamuna flowed close to this hill in that age.

At this time Delhi, the capital of the Tughlaq Sultans, was a walled city known as Jahanpana, the north western gate of which opened on the Hauz-i-Khas; it lay six miles due south of the centre of the modern Connaught Circus. There was no habitation on the vast tract north and east of it, which were later covered by Old Delhi or Purana Qila of Sher Shah, Mughal Delhi or Shah Jahanabad, and New Delhi of the British regime. It should be remembered that the Jamuna in 1398 flowed two miles *west* of its present bed, by the side of the now ruined capital of the Khilji and Tughlaq kings. The low-lying land between the city and the river used to be flooded every year in the rainy season, and when in September the water receded, a wild jungle of *Jhau, babul*, and other shrubs sprang up there. This tract lay as a vast wilderness, broken only by a few stray huts of the nomadic shepherds (Gujars) and hermits' groves.

His Encampment

On 9th December, Timur crossed the Jamuna to the east bank by a ford at Palla (a village 6 miles east of the Narela railway station, and now two miles west of the Jamuna bed). From the crossing place he marched ten miles south along the east bank and established his base at Loni, a large town nine miles north-east of the nearest point in Shah Jahan's Delhi on the west bank. This Loni was a grand mart where the grain from the fertile Ganga-Jamuna Doab used to be collected for sale to the capital across the river. Moreover, there were rich

[1] Pak Pattan, 70 m. e. of Talamba, while Dipalpur is 28 m. n. e. of P. Pattan. Bhatner, 75 m. s. e. of P. Pattan, Sirsa, 44 m. due e. of Bhatner. Tohana, 55 m. n. e. of Sirsa. Samana, 45 m. n. e. of Sirsa. Panipat, 70 m. s. e. of Samana (in straight lines)

pastures around it, which could feed the invader's horses and camels, while the Delhi side was arid and barren. For this reason, 360 years later, Ahmad Shah Durrani halted with his army in the Doab for one year, before recrossing the Jamuna and fighting the Marathas at Panipat.

On the 12th of the month Timur led a small party of 700 armour-clad horsemen down to another ford below Loni, where he crossed over to the Delhi side to reconnoitre and choose a site for delivering battle. After looking out from the Jahannuma hillock, as he was returning, a Delhi force of 4,000 horse, 5,000 foot and 75 elephants attacked his rear-guard of 300 cavalry. The Turks being outnumbered retreated fighting and thus drew their enemies nearer to the ford. Timur sent up reinforcements from the east bank, who completely routed the Delhi force after assailing it with arrows and then charging again and again, and pursued the fugitives to the walls of Delhi.

On the 14th Timur shifted his camp from Loni to a place on the same bank opposite the north point of the modern Red Fort, after massacring the lakh of Hindu prisoners collected in his camp, lest they should endanger his safety while he was engaged in his battle with the Delhi Sultan.

Next day, leaving one man out of every ten to guard his camp and baggage on the east bank, he crossed over to the west bank with his fighting force, and pitched his camp between the river and the Pahari hillock. The Turkish soldiery had been seized with terror from the current stories of the ferocity and power of the Indian war-elephants, which were said to twine their trunk round an armour-clad trooper and hurl him with his horse into the air. Timur took extraordinary precautions to counter the offensive of these beasts and thus heartened his men. Immediately after reaching his camping ground, he ordered his captains to concentrate their men round his own tents, so as to form a small compact circle, easier to defend. The periphery of the camp was divided among his captains and each of them immediately set to digging a deep trench in front of his own sector. Trees were cut down and their branches used in forming an *abatis* behind the trench. Where the nature of the ground did not allow digging, planks were set up to complete the line of circumvallation.[1] The many hundreds of buffaloes seized during the campaign and used as draught-animals, were placed behind the *abatis*, with their necks and feet tied together. So also were the camels. These were most effective steps in breaking any charge of the elephants.

This work being completed in six hours, by captains and common soldiers working shoulder to shoulder, Timur rode round inspecting the line, and then ordered a strict watch to be kept all night and every officer to remain at his appointed place. But no night-attack was attempted from the Indian side, though the Karaunas then ruling at Delhi belonged to a race famous for their skill in making surprises and ambuscades; they knew that the Turkish night watches on superb horses were patrolling round Timur's camp.

Timur's force was counted at Samana as 72,000 horsemen. Since then he had had no casualties, and therefore in the battle of Delhi he had at least 55,000 (more probably 60,000) first-rate cavalry at his command. The Delhi Sultan's Wazir Mallu Khan had only 10,000 cavalry followed by 40,000 infantry and 120 elephants.[2] These foot soldiers were rustics taken from the plough, Jats, Gujars and Meo robbers; their favourite weapon was the bamboo staff, though many of them carried a rusty sword also. There were archers among them, but the Indian bow could not pierce like the famous bow of Central Asia, and their arrows were stopped by the armour and even the leather-coats of the Turkish horsemen. Years of civil war and disorder had made the Delhi Government too poor to maintain a large army or to properly equip what men they entertained. Their sole reliance was on the herd of elephants trained in war and famous for their power as rank-breakers (*saf-shikan*) and cavalry-dispersers.

[1] The Zafar-namah of S. Yezdi says (Bib. Ind. ed. p. 96).—"He made a fort with the branches of trees and chappar (thatch) and placed the buffaloes before the ditch." Not supported by Timur's autobiography.

[2] Akbarnamah (Eng. tr. I. 244) Sharfuddin Yezdi's Zafarnamah (Pers. text, I. 83).

Battle of Delhi

The night of 15th December passed in peace. Next morning Timur ordered his generals to marshal their ranks. After inspecting them, he sent his vanguard ahead to reconnoitre. Two Indians captured by them gave him news about the enemy's strength and disposition, Soon afterwards the Delhi army was sighted in the distance advancing to combat. Timur rode up to the top of a near-by hillock, surveyed the field with his eagle glance, and returning to his place in his battle line gave the order to advance.

Timur's army was drawn up in the regular Turki plan which continued to be followed up to the last days of the Delhi Empire under Babur's dynasty. There were five main divisions,—the Vanguard (*harawal*), the Right Wing (*baranghar*), the Left Wing (*jaranghar*), the Centre (*Kul* or *Ghol*) and the Rear-guard (*chandawal*). In front spread a line of mounted skirmishers (*qarawal*). But the most useful corps was the *iltmish* or advanced Reserve, posted on the two flanks of the centre, just clear of the rear of the Right and Left wings, or sometimes in front of them. This *iltmish*, by its timely addition of fresh troops and its dashing gallantry, very often turned the scale in dubious battles. In the typical Turkish battles, at the outer end of each wing a body of agile light cavalry was placed to make a *detour* (*taulqama*) round the enemy's flank and take him in the rear, when in Gibbon's words "the two horns of the crescent closed in the rear."

Timur's van and wings were commanded by high-spirited princes of his house (his grandsons), supported by old and experienced generals, while he himself took post under the great imperial banner in the Centre, whence he sent off adjutants directing the tide of battle. The Delhi army was thus drawn up: the Right Wing under Malik Muin-ud-din, the Left under Taghi Khan, the Centre under the Sultan (Mahmud Tughluq) with his Wazir Mallu Khan, and the rearguard. His 120 elephants were spread out before the entire front line.

Timur's plan was to make an oblique attack and first disperse the enemy's vanguard and left wing, and therefore he delayed action against the Delhi centre and right,—probably because[1] their left front was not so well protected by elephants and the road to Delhi lay along the right of the advancing Turks, so that it was easier for Timur to make a detour by that side than by the broken eastern or riverward flank. Therefore, when setting his troops in motion he first pushed up his *iltmish* to strengthen his van and right, and issued tactical instructions to all his divisional commanders.

As the Delhi army came up beating its drums and cymbals, shouting and raising clouds of dust, a select body of Turki horsemen detached itself from the van, and making a detour to their own right hand, secretly behind the scrub, took the Delhi Vanguard in the rear, scattered it by their sudden charge and slew 600 of the men. Next his Right Wing fell upon the Delhi Left. The Turki heavy cavalry by their showers of arrows threw the enemy into disorder and then attacked sword in hand. The Indian elephants were boldly tackled, their drivers shot down, and even the trunk of one beast cut off by Timur's grandson! This wing broke and fled away.

By this time Timur's left wing had engaged the Indian Right, which also was broken after a vigorous fight and pursued to the gates of Delhi. Meantime, the Indian centre had boldly advanced to attack Timur's main division, the Centre, driving a line of fierce war elephants before it. Its two flanks were uncovered by the defeat and flight of both wings, while fresh troops pushed up by Timur from his rear arrived to stiffen his fighting centre. Timur now gave his finishing stroke; he sent up the royal bodyguards from his own side to cut their way through the confused crowd of fighters and fugitives before them and reinforce the front line.

The end is best described in the conqueror's own words:—"They brought the elephant-drivers down to the ground with their arrows and killed them. Then they attacked and wounded the elephants with their swords. The soldiers of Sultan Mahmud and Mallu Khan showed no lack of courage, but bore themselves manfully in the fight; still they could not with-

[1] As Timur in advancing kept touch with his entrenched camp in his left rear, his battle front was not parallel to that of the Indians, but his right extreme struck the left extreme of the Delhi force at an acute angle. The battle began with an oblique attack due to natural causes.

stand the successive assaults of my soldiers. Seeing their own plight . . . their courage fell and they took to flight."

Next Delhi humbly submitted to Timur, but the city was sacked and its people massacred by his soldiers for four days together. This victory was followed by a campaign in the Doab of which the most remarkable feature was the success of the Turkish horsemen in overcoming Indian resistance in boats and river islands; though the Turks had no flotilla of their own, their arrows proved most effective long-range missiles in crushing the stationary Indians.

CHAPTER VII

BABUR'S INVASION: FIRST PANIPAT, 1526

A hundred and twenty-five years after Timur's invasion, his sixth descendant in the direct male line, Zahiruddin Babur began the Turki conquest of India. Babur had led an adventurous life with much fighting and many reverses ever since the age of twelve, but shown wonderful tenacity in recovering his own. At last losing his paternal dominion, the small State of Fargana, he had established himself in Kabul (1505), and from this base he began a series of raids into the Panjab which was then governed by Daulat Khan on behalf of the Lodi Sultan of Delhi. Daulat was faithless to his master and courted Babur in the hope of making himself independent, but in the end his ally crushed him and seized the Panjab for himself (1525). Next year Babur marched into Hindustan to found a new empire at Delhi which his descendants held till 1857.

Ibrahim Lodi, the Afghan Sultan of Delhi (accession in 1517) was a brave man; but his government was torn by the rebellions of his kinsmen who fought and conspired to make themselves independent in their respective districts or to oust him from the throne. To these constant dissensions was added what Babur calls "the rustic stupidity" of the Afghans, so that no effective stand could be made by them against Babur's hardy seasoned troops organised in strict discipline and orderly gradation and led by a military genius of the first rank.

From Lahore Babur marched rapidly to Panipat, capturing the Lodi posts on the way and defeating two detachments sent by Ibrahim in advance of himself, one north-west of Delhi and the other eastwards into the Doab.

Against such a swift-paced compact enemy force, Ibrahim Lodi moved in the lordly Indian fashion, making one march of two or three miles and then halting for two days. His camp was one vast disorderly moving city. It was an exact precursor of the march of Emperor Muhammad Shah's army to meet

Ahmad Shah Durrani in 1747, as graphically described by Anandram Mukhlis. At last he contacted Babur's army which had reached Panipat on 12th April, 1526. The decisive battle was fought eight days later, and during this interval there were only skirmishes between patrols.

The Rival Forces

Babur's strength in this battle is not definitely stated in his *Memoirs*. The court historian of Akbar says that it was 12,000 cavalry, but that must have been the number of his choice Turkish horsemen or first-class troops. To these we must add his foot musketeers and Indian allies, as well as the hordes of Afghan and Turki adventurers drawn to his standard by the lure of gold. Lt-Col. Wolseley Haig estimates Babur's forces in this battle at 25,000 men.

Ibrahim Lodi's army was reported in popular rumour to be one lakh of men and one thousand war elephants. These round numbers are manifestly inflated and require severe reduction. A Government distracted by years of civil war and local rebellion, had not money enough to keep a lakh of good cavalry, and Babur himself admits that Ibrahim's miserliness (more correctly his State bankruptcy) had prevented him from increasing his forces by hiring *sehbandi* or militia men for this battle. It would be a fair conjecture to number the Delhi army as 20,000 well-equipped State cavalry and 20,000 baronial levies, mounted on sorry country horses. Behind these were a motley crowd of some 30,000 foot soldiers, retainers and other classes, some armed with pikes and swords, most with bows, and many with bamboo rods only, like the Jat peasant recruits.

On Babur's side there were fire-arms, an absolutely new weapon in North Indian warfare.

Babur drew up his forces east of the town of Panipat, with his face to the south. His front was protected by a laager of 700 baggage carts, the wheels of every two being tied together in the Turki fashion with ropes of raw ox-hide, instead of iron chains. Between every two carts (about 16 yards) five or six shields (called mantlets) on wooden tripods were set up, behind which match-lockmen were to stand when firing. His right flank was protected by its joining the houses of Panipat town, and his left flank was defended by ditches—which I take to mean the dried *nalas* of the Jamuna river which had receded eastwards after the monsoon floods. Where there was no such natural protection he planted *abatis* with branches cut from the abundant jungle of that region. At distances of an arrow's flight sally-places were left open in the laager for a hundred or more horsemen to pass through. At that time the bed of the Jamuna was only two miles east of Panipat and not ten miles as now.

Babur's army was divided into vanguard, left wing, right wing, and centre. He commanded the centre, riding in its main mass with separate divisions on his own right and left flanks. Besides these there were two bodies of select Turkish horsemen at the outer ends of the right and left wings, whose task it was to turn the enemy's flanks and take him in the rear, this tactic being known by the Turki word *taulqama* or "the horns of the crescent closing in the enemy's rear." In addition to these divisions, there were two smaller bodies known as the *iltmish* or easily disposable reserve, placed near the two shoulders of the centre; their duty was to go promptly and reinforce any hard-pressed wing. These arrangements had been practised during his march for some days before, so that there was no delay or confusion in each soldier taking up his appointed place on the day of battle.

The Delhi army set out in battle array from its camp at break of day and covered the intervening four miles in three hours. Babur's men, falling in at the first news of the enemy's advance, waited in calm confidence for the encounter. The enemy's movements indicating that they intended to attack Babur's right wing first, he promptly pushed reinforcements up to it. The Afghans at first advanced swiftly onwards, but on coming close enough to see Babur's front line defences, they abruptly checked themselves, being uncertain what to do next. Their pace slackened and they lost the advantage of a shock charge. The sudden halt in their front ranks threw the long tail of their army into disorder.

At this moment Babur struck. His turning parties made a

detour on the right and the left and on reaching the enemy's rear began to rain arrows on their dense masses. At the same time his right and left wings advanced and engaged the enemy before them at close quarters. The elephants on which the Indians chiefly relied proved of no use; their drivers were shot down or galled with arrows and the beasts wounded and forced to turn back, treading down their own men. The attack on Babur's right wing was pressed home with desperate courage, in order to sever his connection with the city of Panipat, turn his flank through this gap and reach the main body of his troops, avoiding his laager and guns in front. But he repeatedly pushed fresh troops into this wing and here also the Afghan attack failed.

In the next stage of the battle Babur's centre engaged the enemy centre, preventing it from sending any help to its own hard-pressed wings. The matchlockmen of Ustad Ali Quli (centre front) and the carted guns of Mustafa Khan Rumi (left of the centre) worked havoc among the densely crowded Afghan ranks. The Indian army was now entirely surrounded and pushed back into a disordered circle. The Afghans fought with the desperate fury of trapped beasts: some of their captains even attempted counter-charges here and there. But it was all in vain; the mischief of wrong tactics and inferior arms could not be remedied, though six thousand of their men fell in a circle round their dead king Ibrahim Lodi. Then their host broke up in flight; a relentless pursuit followed in which slaughter, plunder and abduction were carried to the very gates of Delhi. Pyramids were built with the heads of the slain; Timur's example was followed by his great-grandson's grandson.

Early Fire-Arms

There is much confusion of thought on the subject of the early use of fire-arms in India and many ludicrous statements have found a place in our books in consequence of it. All this is due to our writers' failure to distinguish between *fire-works* and *fire-arms*, or in other words between combustible and explosive agents. Fire-arms truly so-called must have the propelling power of their shot in some explosive substance, their missile must not be hurled by the hand, or by some dart-throwing machine. Secondly, they must discharge some solid projectile which will penetrate and not merely burn. Missiles that merely burn have been in use in the world's history from long before the Christian era; such were the Greek fire (a combustible substance which water cannot quench), fire-balls (that are ignited cotton balls steeped in oil, resin or naphtha and tied to the point of an arrow and shot into the enemy ranks), or even live coal or burning sulphur put in a pot and thrown by the hand like a rugby ball.

These were not fire-arms. Nor can that name be applied to the old rockets (*hawai*), fire-wheels (*charkhi*) and squibs (*pataka*) which our boys set off on Diwali nights. Though gunpowder is used in making them, they are merely fire-works. They can start a fire though not in every case, but not penetrate any obstacle. Another defect of these fire-works when used in war is that their direction of flight and accuracy of aim are entirely left to chance. Such fire-works had been in use among the Afghans of Bengal from before Babur's invasion, evidently learnt from the Portuguese mariners, or even the Chinese. Babur vaguely describes them, when he writes of his victory over the Afghans in Bihar—"Bengalis have a reputation for fire-working, (*atish bazi*); we tested it now; they do not fire counting to hit a particular spot, but fire at random." (*Tuzuk*, p. 672).

For accuracy of aim and penetration, the missile has to be a solid metal ball or stone, inserted in a long tube and its propelling power created by the explosion of gun-powder in a closed chamber behind the shot. Thus the gun originated. The guns were of two kinds: for smaller missiles and shorter ranges, straight shooting (with a low trajectory) was necessary, hence the hand-gun now known as the musket. But for heavy missiles intended for smashing obstacles, vertical firing was necessary: hence the origin of the big howitzer (called mortar). One big gun used by the Ottoman Turks at the siege of Constantinople in 1453, fired stone balls weighing 700 lbs. Babur's Persian Chief of Ordnance in 1526 cast an iron mortar at Agra which sent a stone shot 1,600 paces, or 1,400 yards, three-fourths of a mile.

Babur's fire-arms at Panipat consisted solely of hand-guns and light pieces resting on forks (falconets), because he had transported his weapons from Kabul on the backs of camels. He had no mortar with him, because as he says, "Three or four elephants have gone dragging without trouble the carriage of a mortar which it takes four or five hundred men to haul." (*Memoirs*, p. 489). His only large mortar was cast by Ustad Ali Quli at Agra in October 1526, and first used in the battle of Khanwa,—where (I believe) it was fired not more than thrice in the whole course of the day. It burst after firing on 24th November, 1527.

In the earlier stages, the field-guns or artillery proper had no wheeled carriage for each piece, but a number of them were carried together in one ordinary baggage transport cart. This was the case with Babur.

The hand-gun came into practical use in Europe in 1446, and was of a very rude construction. It consisted of a simple iron or brass tube fixed in a *straight* stock of wood and having a touch-hole bored at the *top*. A match for firing it was made of cotton or hemp spun slack, and boiled in a strong solution of saltpetre. Afterwards the touch-hole was placed at the *side* of the barrel, with a small pan underneath to hold the priming powder. These guns were at first called *hand-culverins* and weighed about 10 lbs., throwing leaden bullets of an ounce or so. In the latter part of the 15th century the hand-gun was made into a *matchlock* by the addition of a cock to hold the match and a trigger to bring it down on the powder-pan. The stock was also curved so that the piece could be aimed and fired from the shoulder. These were called *harquebus* in France and *hackbutt* in England, and their length was only three feet, with a very short range.

In 1520 the Spaniards developed the musket, which at first meant a weapon six feet long, weighing about 15 lbs. and firing a two ounce bullet with an effective range of 400 paces. The barrel rested on a portable fork at the time of firing. "The unwonted penetration of their bullets disordered the ranks of their enemy's men at arms. The Spanish musketeers were broken up into small parties, which moved about rapidly, giving turns and making volte-faces here and there from one side to another."

The rockets (*ban*) used in Babur's time continued to be very popular with the Asiatic armies, especially the Marathas and the fighting monks of Rajputana, called Naga Sannyasis and Vairagis. These monks boasted that at the battle of Tunga (1787) they shot 35 rockets into Mahadji Sindhia's army (which was fighting with De Boigne's improved artillery). These rockets (*ban*) must not be confounded with the *hawai* which are set off at modern marriages and Diwali celebrations. Their flight was most erratic, and whether their shot fell on the enemy or was thrown by the recoil among the friends behind, depended entirely on chance. In fact, their only effect was to frighten raw infantry, cause a stampede among horses, and very rarely set fire to the enemy's munitions or tents by one lucky shot in a thousand. Humayun's fire-arms at the battle of Bilgram (1540) are thus described by Mirza Haider Dughlat (*Tarikh-i-Rashidi*, Eng. tr. by Elias, p. 474):—

> "Among the equipments of the Emperor were 700 carts (*gardun*) each drawn by four pairs of bullocks and carrying a swivel (*Zarb-zan*) which fired a ball of 500 *misqals* (4-1/2 lbs.) weight. They would strike anything that was visible at the distance of a *parasang* (3 miles)."

Among Akbar's improvements of his fire-arms were the greater use of wheeled carriages for his artillery, the lengthening of the barrel of the hand-musket (reaching 6 feet 3-1/4 inches in total length), and the increase of "harquebuses on forks," i.e., resting on a hook fixed in a wall or a frame on the back of an elephant or a camel (called *ganjnal* and *shutarnal*). "These wall-pieces sometimes weighed as much as 50 lbs. and had bullets of 3 or 4 oz. weight" (Lloyd's *Review of the History of Infantry*, 90-91 *Encyclo. Brit.* 11th ed. Vol. 12, pp. 717, Vol. 2, pp. 685-686; Irvine's *Army of the Indian Moguls;* Abul Fazl's *Akbarnamah;* Blochmann's tr., Vol. I; Egerton, *Handbook of Indian Arms*. For the *Greek fire*, see Bury's note in his edition of Gibbon's *Decline and Fall*, Vol. vi, p. 540 (Appendix) and Omar's *Art of War in M. Ages*, 1st. ed., 546.)

CHAPTER VIII

BABUR AND RANA SANGA, 1527

The battle of Khanwa was the supreme test of Babur's generalship. His soldiers marched to it disheartened by defeat in patrol actions, terrified by stories of Rajput valour and astrologers' prediction of adverse stars, and weakened by the desertion of timid allies. Facing him was an enemy more than double his own numbers and flushed with unbroken success. If he was defeated or even forced to retreat after a drawn fight, the shock of his failure would shatter his new-born empire of Delhi to pieces. But he had one weapon which the Rajputs could not match, these were his mortars and matchlocks, which were then absolutely unknown in North India. Above all shone his military genius and experience of war earned by incessant fights since the age of twelve. On the Rajput side there was valour no doubt, but no generalship, no brain in the directing staff, no cohesion of the parts.

Babur's Precautions

In this campaign Babur advanced to the decisive battle step by step, guarding his camp and men and fortifying his position every evening, so as to defeat any night attack and also to ensure a safe base in the event of a forced retreat. His battle formation also looked like a fortified encampment, *minus* its ditch (for which there was no place in a moving field, but possessed of a mobility in its defence tools impossible in a fortress).

Babur's plan of battle at Khanwa was to turn his army front into a fort or laager of carts guarded by fire-arms, and to sit tight there during the first stage and break by his matchlock-fire and stone-hurling mortars wave after wave of Rajput assault till the assailants were decimated and worn out and their leaders slain. When that final stage came and the enemy ranks were found shaken, he would assume the offensive and come out of his laager. That was exactly the situation at the close of Waterloo, when Wellington gave the order, "The whole line will now advance." Therefore, after drawing up his line of battle Babur isued strict commands to all his captains not to make any move nor to allow any soldier to take one step out of his position except on order from himself. The Bakhshi (field-marshal) stood by his side and sent out couriers and aides to convey Babur's orders to the different commanders with every change in the tide of battle.

Tactics Of The Battle

For the first three hours, the only hand-to-hand fighting was on the two wings, on their extreme ends unprotected by fire-arms, while the Mughal centre kept the enemy back by gunfire, to which the Rajputs had no missile reply. The superior numbers of the Rajputs and the terror inspired by their early successes over Babur's detachments, held him back from turning the enemy's flanks by his favourite *taulqama* or pincer movement.

A treacherous desertion at the outset upset Rana Sanga's pre-arranged plan of combat. Silhadi, a Rajput adventurer, who had made himself master of Raisin and Sarangpur, and often changed sides during that troubled time, had lately turned Muslim to save his estate but joined Sanga with his contingent (30,000 on paper, but probably not more than 6,000 in muster). He went over to Babur's side from his post in the vanguard (left wing) of the Hindu army. This misfortune enforced a hurried consultation and change of plan on the Rana, and the issue of new orders to his divisions. The second disaster to the Rajputs came when the Rana lost consciousness from a severe wound. This event I am inclined took place in the fourth hour of the battle (about 1 p.m.), when Babur noticed "the accursed infidels to remain confounded for one hour," which means that there was a lull in the fighting; it was also the time for the second or great *namaz* of the day (when fighting always slackens). At the end of this lull, the desperate Rajputs, abandoning the love of life set out on their famous last "death ride," which ended in their destruction. The supreme commander's collapse was concealed by the inner circle of the Rajput commanders, who continued the fight with a counterfeit Sanga (really a Jhala chieftain) seated on the royal elephant. This arrangement took some time to effect, during which the Rajputs made no attack. (*Vir Vinod*, i. 366; *Mirat-i-Sikandari* for Silhadi).

The Rival Forces

In the morning of the battle (17th March, 1527) Babur drew up his forces in the following order:—First, the baggage-carts of the army (700 at Panipat, probably 1,000 at Khanwa), were placed in one line in front about 40 feet apart, but tied together in the Turki fashion with thongs cut out of raw hide (for want of iron chains). Between every two carts, five or six movable shields (in European war called *mantlets*), fixed to wheeled tripods, were placed, behind which the musketeers sheltered when firing. In the line of linked carts, openings were left at distances of an arrow's flight (about 60 yards) for a hundred horsemen to sally out. The mortars, falconets (small field-guns), and foot-musketeers formed the second line behind the carts. In the third line stood the regular heavy cavalry, his main weapon of attack.

Ustad Ali Quli was posted in front of the centre with his mortar and other wheeled guns, or what was called the *Jinsi topkhana* under the Mughal empire, while his rival Mustafa Khan (a Turk from Asia Minor), stood apart from him, in front of the centre of the right wing, with his musketeers and swivel-guns (*Zamburak*), or the *Dasti topkhana* of later days. The cavalry was formed into three main divisions,—the right wing (under Prince Humayun, probably 5,000 strong), the left wing (under Mahdi Khwaja, probably 3,000) and the centre (under Babur himself, about 10,000 strong) with his own detachable left and right flanks. In addition to these, there were two bodies of specially chosen cavalry not more than a thousand each,—which I may call commando troops—posted at the extreme ends of the two wings, for dealing the famous Turkish blow of *taulqama* by turning the enemy's flanks and taking him in the rear. We read of no special reserve (*iltmish* in Turki), nor of any rearguard, nor vanguard distinct from the centre front. The Indian allies of Babur were posted in his left wing, which had a good deal of its front uncovered by fire-arms.

As the Rajputs surged up towards Babur's centre in a vast tumultuous shouting crowd, they saw before them a flash like lightning, then a roar of thunder, and lastly a huge hot stone ball came hurtling through the air like a burning meteor, which hit them at a range of six furlongs and crushed everything in its path. Even elephants could not stand before it. It was the first shot from Ustad Ali-Quli's mortar cast only six months before. Those Rajputs who had galloped up closer to the front were stabbed by small fire-flashes which vomited a hail storm of burning slugs and stone chips spreading like grape-shot through their ranks. These were the musket-bullets. The Rajputs had never seen anything like it before. Their advance upon the centre was stopped for the rest of the day and they tried to probe the enemy's wings instead.

"When guns were first used the noise they made on discharge must have produced a bewildering fear in those without previous experience of them; more especially would this be the case with horses and other animals.... There is always the ever-present fear that the stroke will fall without giving any evidence of whence it came." (*Encyclop. Brit.* xx. 189).

Thus both armies operated only on the flanks,—the Rajputs because they could not advance against the thunder and lightning in front of them, and Babur because he was wise enough not to throw away the advantage of his stationary line of carts and musketeers, which alone could stop the impetuous rush of the Rajput desperadoes and their infuriated elephants whereas if his horsemen had been advanced into the open plain at this stage, before the enemy had been decimated and convulsed, his army would have been swallowed up in the ocean of the Rajput cavalry and his fire masked by his own men.

Rajput Attack How Met

The Rajputs durst not assault the fortress-looking centre, but galloped upon the two wings, driving their elephants in front. The first impact was on the Mughal right wing, but Babur's eagle eye detected their plan and he at once pushed up reinforcements to this wing, which repulsed the attack, while its right hand section and *taulqama* corps by a counter-attack pushed the Rajputs back almost to the rear of their own centre. The Rajputs came up again in another wave of assault. By this time their disposition and distances having become known, Mustafa Khan opened fire upon them with his match-locks. Still the Rajputs continued fighting in broken groups, but Babur sent up fresh troops in support of his men. As his secretary describes the scene, "Band after band of pagan troops followed each other to help their men, so we in our turn sent detachment after detachment to reinforce our fighters on that side."

Simultaneously with this first attack, the left wing of Babur was charged by the Rajput right. Here also desperate fighting took place, the combat ebbing and flowing as each side reinforced its men. In the end Babur's left wing commando (*taulqama*) strengthened by additions from the vanguard, counter-charged and penetrated as far as the Rajput rear. But at this stage, the pincer movement was not completed, "the two horns of the crescent" did not close, and Babur's men rode back to their own posts. More and more troops were sent from Babur's centre to meet the enemy pressure on this wing which was originally very weak in number.

In the centre the Rajputs continued to fall without being able to retaliate in the least or advance to close grips. They were hopelessly outclassed in weapons and their dense masses only increased their helpless slaughter, as every bullet found its billet.

Babur's Final Advance

This ding-dong fighting went on from 10 o'clock in the morning till half past twelve, when Babur saw that the time had come for him to assume the offensive. He let loose his choice guard corps so long kept in reserve behind the carts, "like tigers held back by leashes," (as his secretary well describes them). They sallied out of the laager by the two open lanes on the right and left of the line of musketeers in the centre and fell on the enemy's centre from two sides. Next the matchlockmen of the Mughal centre issued from their shelter and attacked the Rajputs in front, doing havoc at close range. Finally the wheeled artillery was advanced and Babur himself followed them with his centre into the thick of the fight, his men swarming around him on all sides "like the waves of a surging ocean." A mingled combat now ensued under clouds of dust and universal confusion, for about an hour. But steadily the Rajputs were pushed back, most of their captains who had rushed to the front to hearten their men fell, and even the supreme commander Rana Sanga was removed from the field senseless from his wounds.[1]

Heavy Slaughter

The last duty of Hindu warriors had now to be performed. The Rajputs made a desperate charge on the right and left flanks only as before; but here their bravest were mown down and the battle ended in their irretrievable defeat. The remnant of their army dispersed "like carded wool" leaving heaps of dead on the stricken field. The wounded perished as they lay on the ground or fell down from exhaustion during flight. "Countless numbers of the bodies of Rajputs and their Muslim allies encumbered the road as far as Biana, and even beyond it towards Alwar and Mewat."

The victors marched into the Rana's camp, four miles ahead of Babur's last halting place. But no relentless pursuit was possible after the long and dubious struggle, and daylight also failed soon after its end. Babur gave up the idea of invading Mewar, because of the mid-summer heat and the want of water and fodder on the way.

[1] The wound is said to have been inflicted by an arrow (*tir*). I take it to be a bullet (*tir-i-tufang*), because the word *tir* is used in both senses.

CHAPTER IX

HUMAYUN VS. SHER SHAH

Napoleon once remarked, "In war it is not men that count, but *the man*", The truth of this saying is best illustrated by the career of Sher Shah Sur. Within ten years of Babur's death, his son Humayun lost his Indian empire through sheer incapacity and weakness of character, though he had succeeded to the command of his father's ever-victorious troops and the vast resources of the empire of Delhi. From a petty jagirdar's cast-off son Sher made himself by his supreme capacity for war and administration alike and his genius for managing men, first the head of the Afghans in South Bihar and next of Bengal, and finally the conqueror of the Delhi throne. Humayun was defeated by him in two decisive battles,—Chausa (26 June, 1539) and Bilgram (17 May, 1540) and driven out of India, and Sher Shah ruled in his place for the rest of his life (1540—1545).

The Turks are natural soldiers, but they can fight only under good leadership, as Osman Pasha was to prove at Plevna (1877). Humayun was no leader. His character was a contrast to his father's. A good-natured man, he lacked the iron will, the unrelaxed vigour, and the ruthless instinct of his nomad ancestors. The opium habit and the self-indulgent life of the richest monarch in Asia had sapped what little tenacity of will and decision of character he ever possessed, though he retained his personal courage to the last. His officers, once the glory of Babur's army, had mostly perished in the Indian climate and the rest had begun to abandon him in despair. Thus when the conflict with Sher Shah came, his soldiers proved a flock of sheep without a shepherd, upon whom the Indo-Afghans fell with the speed and ferocity of wolves. No stand was made by the Mughal soldiers; taken utterly by surprise, most of them unaccoutred, and all in disarray and without any leader, they merely took to flight and perished in the river, unwounded by the enemy. Hence, these two battles have nothing to teach the military student except what *not* to do in war.

Chausa, 26th June, 1539

On 16th August 1538, Humayun wrested from Sher Shah's agent the city of Gaur, the then capital of Bengal. Here he spent six months in the enjoyment of ease and pleasure, while many of his soldiers were killed by the pestilential climate and most of those that remained alive were enervated. When at last he set out on return to Agra, he found his path hemmed round by Sher Shah's moving bands in full control of the country. So, he came to a halt at Chausa (10 miles south-west of Buxar) on the frontier between Bihar and Banaras, at the end of March, 1539. For nearly three months he lay encamped in the fork between the Ganges in the north and the Karamnasa river in the west. Disease, hardship, and fear of the enemy prompted many of his soldiers to desert for their homes, and he opened negotiations with Sher Shah.

Then in the early morning of 26th June Sher Shah struck with consummate skill. He first of all deluded his enemies by signing a peace treaty and then threw them totally off their guard by undertaking a campaign against his local Hindu enemy, the Chero chieftain Maharatha. One large division of his army under Khawas Khan was sent away to attack the Chero strongholds far to the south, and on two successive nights Sher himself with the bulk of his army marched out of camp as if to support this column, but he used to return in the morning. Thus his troops were accustomed to making night marches in silence and without delay or disorder. On the third night, after leaving his camp, he marched at first for five miles away from Humayun's position, then halted, divulged to his troops his plan of surprising Humayun's camp that very night, and being joined by Khawas Khan as pre-arranged, he took a sharp turn eastwards, crossed the river unperceived some five miles below Humayun's position and then riding due north penetrated the sleeping Mughal camp from three sides at the break of day. The surprise was complete; Humayun saved himself by abandoning all his artillery baggage and women to the enemy.

Eight thousand Mughals perished, and "the Mughal army was practically destroyed."

Bilgram, 17th May, 1540

Humayun's next encounter with Sher Shah was at a place opposite the city of Kanauj, but some three miles distant from the bank of the Ganges, and near Bilgram. It was not a battle at all but a helpless panic flight, which covered the Mughals with unspeakable disgrace. I can best describe it in the words of Mirza Haidar Dughlat, who commanded one of the divisions of Humayun's army on that day.

The Mughal camp being situated on a low-lying tract which the monsoon rains began to flood, it was decided to remove it to a higher ground; but the problem was how to effect the transfer of the vast artillery and other impediments and the tens of thousands of servants, without being attacked by the enemy when disordered by movement.

Mirza Haidar writes—"I suggested that we must keep our forces (drawn up in the field) well under control, until we should see if the enemy came out of his trenches and advanced against us,... in which event a regular pitched battle would be fought with advantage to the Turkish heavy cavalry. The baggage and non-combatants were to be left in the old camp, but if the enemy did not move, these were in the afternoon to move to the new position selected for the camp, and the soldiers would last of all follow and occupy that place.

"On the 10th of Muharram, 947 (17th May, 1540) we mounted to carry the plan into effect. The carriages (swivels) and mortars and small (hand) guns were placed in the centre .... The artillery commanders placed the carriages and mortars in their proper positions, and stretched chains between them. Sher Khan came out in five divisions of 1,000 men each, and in advance of him were 3,000 men... the whole less than 15,000. I calculated the Chaghtai force at about 40,000, all mounted on *kipchak* horses, and clad in iron armour. When Sher Khan's army came out of its entrenchments, two divisions drew up (as the rear or reserve) and three divisions advanced against their opponents. On our side,... when we reached the ground we were unable to occupy it, for every Amir in the Chaghtai army had his camp-followers, a commander of 100 had 500 servants with him. In whatever place there was a conflict, the followers were entirely ungovernable. When they lost their masters they were seized with panic and blindly rushed about.... They so pressed us in the rear that they drove the centre upon the chains stretched between the chariots, and they and the soldiers dashed each other upon them; they broke through the chains, and the men posted by the chains were driven beyond them.... All formation was destroyed.

"Such was the state of the centre. On the right Sher Khan advanced in battle array, but before an arrow was discharged the camp-followers fled like chaff before the wind, and breaking the line, they all pressed towards the centre.... The whole array was broken. While the centre was thus thrown into disorder, all the fugitives from the right bore down upon it. So, before the enemy had discharged an arrow, the whole army was scattered and defeated,—40,000 men fled before 10,000; the Chaghtai were defeated, in this battle-field where not a man, either friend or foe was wounded. Not a gun was fired." Vast numbers were drowned in trying to cross the Ganges,—only eight persons out of one thousand armed retainers in one corps survived. "The total loss may be estimated from this fact." (*Tarikh-i-Rashidi*, Elias tr., p. 475-'77).

This battle proved that the army that cannot take the offensive is doomed, and purely passive defence is futile. "War without strategy is mere butchery."—(*Encyclo. Brit.* 21, p. 840).

Chapter X

SECOND BATTLE OF PANIPAT, 1556

Sher Shah Sur had driven Babur's son Humayun out of India, but within ten years of his death his descendants lost their empire through family quarrels and baronial rebellions. The empire of Delhi shrank into a small kingdom which was torn by disputed succession and the secession of provinces. The last of the Sur kings, Mubariz Khan, Sher's nephew, entitled Muhammad Adil Shah (popularly called 'Adili'), was entirely devoid of energy or capacity and devoted himself solely to the pursuit of pleasure. But his Government gained unwonted strength from his Hindu Minister, Himu Bhargav. This man was a Gaur Brahmin. Though this caste had supplied priests to the Hindu kings of yore, Himu's own family was poor and he made his way up in the Sur royal service by his conspicuous ability for war and civil administration alike. His honesty and devotion to the interests of the State and his strictness in putting down slack and corrupt public servants antagonised the degenerate old official nobility and his memory has been blackened by their false aspersions and the partisan writings of Akbar's court flatterers. Himu, in addition to being a highly efficient civil administrator, was also the best military genius on the Afghan side after Sher Shah's death, far-sighted in his strategic plans, keen-eyed and quick in his tactical decisions, cool in holding his strength in reserve, and fearless of danger in encouraging his troops by his personal example. In the internecine wars of the Afghans, he had fought 22 battles with the domestic enemies of his master and been victorious in all of them.

When Humayun returned from his exile in Persia and recovered Delhi and Agra (23rd July, 1555), Himu marched from the eastern provinces with a large army to recover these royal cities, leaving his master Adili in Chunar fort. Soon afterwards, Humayun died in Delhi on 26th January, 1556.

At the advance of Himu, Humayun's governor of Agra evacuated that city and fled to Delhi. In pursuit of him, Himu reached Tughlaqabad, a village five miles east of the Qutb Minar. Here Tardi Beg, the Mughal governor of Delhi came out and gave him battle on 7th October, against tremendous odds, as Himu was reported to be leading 1,000 elephants, 50,000 horses, 51 cannon and 500 falconets.

The Mughal army was thus drawn up: Abdullah Uzbeg commanded the van, Haidar Muhammad the right wing, Iskandar Beg the left, and Tardi Beg himself the centre. The choice Turki cavalry in the van and left wing attacked and drove back the enemy forces before them, and followed far in pursuit. In this assault the victors captured 400 elephants and slew 3,000 men of the Afghan army. Imagining victory already gained, many of Tardi Beg's followers dispersed to plunder the enemy camp, and he was left in the field very thinly guarded. All this time Himu had been holding 300 choice elephants and a force of select horsemen as a reserve in the centre. He promptly seized the opportunity and made a sudden charge upon Tardi Beg with this reserve. At the impetuous advance of the huge beasts and the dense cavalry behind them, many of the Mughal officers fled away in terror without waiting to offer a defence. At last Tardi Beg himself took the same course.

Himu very wisely did not disperse his troops by attempting a pursuit, but stood in the field with his army drawn up like a solid wall. The victorious Mughal vanguard and left wing, on returning from their chase of their respective opponents, saw that the day had been lost in their absence, and there was no general to rally and lead them; so they dispersed without renewing the fight. Himu now took possession of Delhi city.

The news of the disaster at Tughlaqabad reached the young Emperor Akbar at Jalandhar and he at once set out with all his forces to recover Delhi. The decisive battle was fought on 5th November, 1556, about four miles north-west of the scene of Babur's victory, hence it is called the Second Battle of Panipat. From the way Himu sent forward his advance-guard with the greater part of his artillery to Panipat.

Akbar's advanced division led by Ali Quli Khan Shaibani came upon this force and by combining deceptive cunning with hard-hitting audacity[1] completely deceived and overpowered the blunt Afghans who fled away abandoning their guns, without making any stand.

Undaunted by this initial reverse, Himu advanced to the fight, at the head of 30,000 Rajput and Afghan horsemen, comrades of his former victories. His 500 war elephants were protected by plate armour, and on their backs were placed musketeers and cross-bowmen. The commanders were men of valour and loyalty and proud of their past deeds. But he had no field-gun. Akbar himself then a boy of thirteen, marched with his guardian Bairam Khan twenty miles behind his fighting troops. The battle was fought by ten thousand Mughal cavalry under the command of Ali. Quli Khan (later created Khan-i-Zaman) and without the help of Babur's profuse fire-arms. It was a ding-dong fight, and the heavily outnumbered Mughals would probably have been defeated, if the Afghan side had not lost its leader in the thick of the contest.

The Mughal right wing was under Sikandar Khan Uzbak, the left under Abdullah Khan Uzbak, the centre under Ali Quli Khan Shaibani, and the vanguard under Husain Quli Beg and Shah Quli Mahram (with Bairam's own contingent of Turks). Himu took post in the centre and gave the charge of his right wing to Shadi Khan Kakar and his left to Ramya (his own sister's son).

The battle began with an attack by Himu. The onset of the furious elephants shook the right and left wings of the Mughal army and many hard-fighting warriors fell on their side. The survivors did not flee, but Turk-like withdrew from the frontal fighting to avoid the elephants, and making a detour fell on the enemy horsemen's flanks, galling them with their superior archery and shaking them by their Parthian wheeling tactics. The Mughal centre too advanced, but coming to a plot of ground with a deep ravine in front, which was impassable for elephants, it stood on the defensive plying its mis-

[1] Our "ghazis added feline skill to the deeds of tigers", as Abul Fazl writes, which means a successful ruse followed by a bold demonstration. (*Akbarnamah*, ii. 59).

sile weapons on the foe powerless to reach it with either horse or elephant.

Meanwhile the flanking parties of Turks, mounted on superb horses, had penetrated the enemy ranks from side and rear and were slashing at the elephants' legs or shooting off their drivers. As the Afghan attack slackened and the elephants fell back, Ali Quli led his cavalry out of its shelter and making a detour attacked the Afghan centre from behind. Himu who was surveying the battle field and directing the operations from the back of a lofty elephant, hastened to the threatened side, making every effort to restore the battle and "leaving no stratagem or heroic deed that his mind could conceive unattempted" (*Akbarnamah*, ii. 64). He made repeated counter-charges with his powerful elephants, overthrowing the Mughals in the direct line of his advance. But the war was taking toll of his strength; two of his bravest lieutenants, Bhagwan Das and Shadi Khan Kakar were killed before his eyes. The mixed fighting raged most stubbornly for some time, when an arrow pierced his eye. The blood spouting from the wound was seen by the Afghans near him, but he pulled the arrow out, bandaged the eye with a scarf, and ordered the fight to go on, after which he fell down into the *hauda* in a faint. The fall of the leader ended the battle and the Afghan-Rajput army broke up in hopeless flight.

A Mughal captain seized Himu's elephant and led it away from the battle-field to Akbar's camp, about 8 miles in the rear. Here the half-unconscious champion of the Afghan throne was beheaded by Bairam Khan. Five thousand dead were counted on the field and many more were slain when fleeing.

Chapter XI

MUGHAL CONQUEST OF BENGAL

Battle Of Tukaroi, 1575

The Emperor Akbar, after extending his rule from Delhi and Agra to the middle of northern India, through Oudh and Jaunpur, came up against the north-eastern corner, Bihar and Bengal. This province was then ruled by the Afghan house of Karrani who had seized it during the decline of Sher Shah's dynasty. Sulaiman Karrani (who died in 1572) had wisely saved his throne by professing himself a vassal of Akbar. But his young and hot-headed son Daud Karrani, in foolish pride, cast off his allegiance to Akbar and declared his independence.

An imperial army under Munim Khan (entitled Khan-i-Khanan) advanced into Bihar and laid siege to Patna, in which city Daud had shut himself up with his army. Akbar joined him there on 3rd August, 1574, and three days later took by assault the fort of Hajipur (facing Patna and on the north bank of the Ganges), which victory made Patna untenable. That very night Daud and his generals fled away from Patna in disorder by the land route. Munim Khan gave chase, capturing all the strong places on the way without any resistance, till he reached Tanda (in the Malda district) which was then the capital of Bengal and the latest location of the old historic city of Gaur, on September 25, 1574.

From this base, the Mughal Commander-in-Chief sent out detachments which wrested west, north, central and south Bengal from the local Afghan officers, while their King Daud fled away to Orissa. Thereafter the imperial officers sickened of campaigning in the pestilential climate of Bengal, slackened their exertions; internal dissensions and desertions further weakened them. Munim Khan was too old and weak to control them. So, Akbar sent Raja Todar Mal, as sagacious as brave, with orders to strengthen him and by invading Orissa to crush Daud and put an end to the Afghan menace. Burdwan was made the advance base of the imperial army in Bengal.

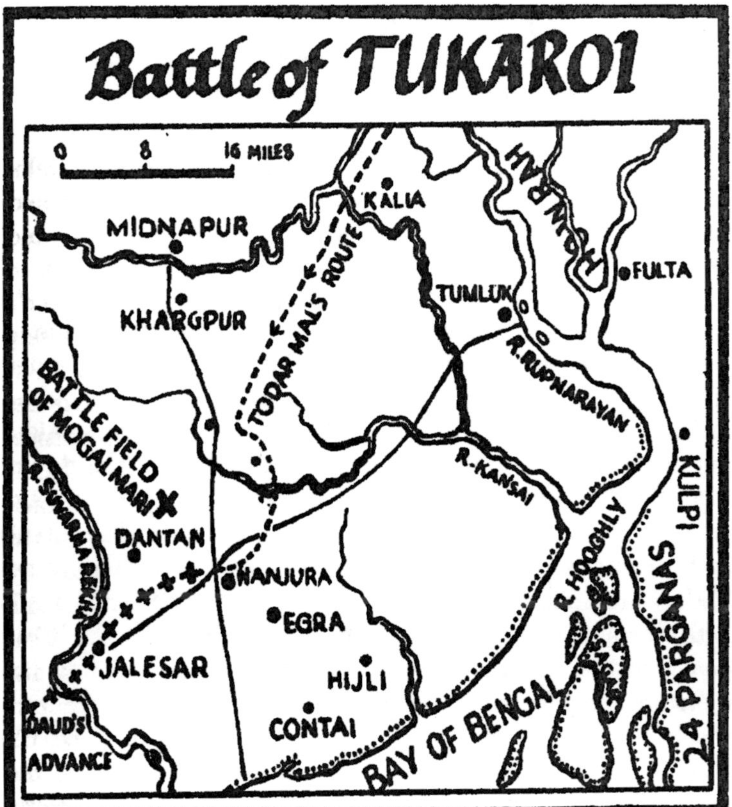

Tukra village of modern map marked as X is Mogalmari in a map of 1840

Meantime Daud returned from Orissa with his army to the Midnapur district to fight the Mughals. Todar Mal advanced from Burdwan to Garh Mandaran (8 miles due west of Arambagh in Hooghly) and thence to Cheto, where Munim Khan joined him with the rest of the imperial army. Daud's position was Garh Haripur, eleven miles south-east of the Dantan railway station. The battle was fought near the village now called Tukra Qasba, nine miles east of Dantan railway station and three miles west of the important village of Nanjura (*Nahanjara* in the latest map). This Nanjura is now two miles west of the modern Midnapur-Contai branch road, being separated from that road by the village of Palasia (some 8 miles north-west of Egra town). But in the days before the railway, the old Midnapur-Contai road passed through Nanjura and the Jalesar-Tamluk road cut the above road only three miles north of Nanjura, (map of 1840). Haripur is also given some 8 miles south-west of it. *Tukra* has been misspelt in Persian writing as *Tukaroi*. There is no reason for calling it the battle of Mughalmari; though the maps give three Mughalmaris in the Jalesar and Midnapur districts, none of them was the site of any major Mughal-Afghan battle, according to history.

Daud had fortified his camp at Haripur by digging a deep trench around it and throwing up breastworks, in Afghan fashion. He had also barricaded the regular road from Midnapur southwards at strategic points, and as this road ran through a jungle the advancing Mughal army could be easily ambushed anywhere on it. The imperial soldiery were disheartened and refused to fight, clamouring for peace with the enemy. Todar Mal and the Khan-i-Khanan harangued and argued with them and cajoled them into a fighting mood. It was dangerous to go straight forward upon Daud's position, and therefore the Mughal chiefs, helped by men with knowledge of the locality, discovered an obscure circuitous path. This route was improved by pioneers, and then the army, making a wide detour by their left, i.e. south-eastwards, arrived at Nanjura, a village close to the Contai-Midnapur road and 11 miles east of Dantan railway station.

Thus Daud's flank was turned and his rear could be cut by the Mughals now after one day's march. He had already sent off his family and *impedimenta* to Katak and lightened his force. He now advanced from his camp to challenge the enemy at their halting place. The encounter took place on the plain of Tukaroi, ten miles south of the angle formed by the B. N. railway line and the branch road from Dantan to Contai.

The Battle Described

The course of the battle can be clearly followed from the Persian histories. The Mughal chiefs had decided not to fight that day, as the stars were inauspicious. They had merely sent out the usual vedettes in front of their camp, when they were surprised to see the enemy rapidly advancing in full force. Munim Khan hurriedly ordered his troops to be drawn up in battle array. He followed the customary formation: the Vanguard (under Alam Khan), the Advanced Reserve or *Iltmish* (under Qiya Khan), the Centre (under Munim Khan), the Left Wing (under Ashraf Khan and Todar Mal), and the Right Wing (under Shaham Khan). But before the imperial army had completed the marshalling of its ranks, Daud precipitated the battle with a furious charge of elephants in a long line under Gujar Khan, upon the Mughal Vanguard. "As the tusks and necks of the elephants were covered with black yak-tails and the skins of the animals, they produced horror and dismay; the horses of the imperial van were frightened on seeing these extraordinary forms, and hearing the terrible cries, and turned back. Though the riders exerted themselves, they were not successful and the troops lost their formation." [*Akbarnamah*, iii. 176]. Khan Alam was slain and his division was scattered. The impetus of the victorious Afghan van similarly broke the imperial *Iltmish* and even swept away the Centre itself. Munim Khan and other officers fought desperately receiving repeated wounds, but their followers "did not behave well". At last, the tide of fugitives swept away the commander-in-chief five miles behind the front. The Afghans of the vanguard, after pursuing him for half a mile, turned aside to plunder his camp; they even went beyond it and dispersed in the attempt to overtake the Mughal camp-followers who were trying to escape with their pack animals.

This ruined the Afghan cause. Daud durst not follow up Gujar Khan's successful charge by pushing into the opening made by him in the Mughal centre and taking the imperial left wing in flank, as he feared that the retreat of the Khan-i-Khanan was merely a ruse for luring him into the jaws of death between his enemies' two wings. The Afghan right wing under

Sikandar merely made a half-hearted frontal demonstration against the Mughal left wing, and then "fled without coming to blows", because here Todar Mal and other officers held their ground firmly and presented a bold front. When Daud himself arrived in support of his right wing he could do no better. Meantime the severely shaken Mughal divisions had been rallied; everywhere brave men had formed themselves into small knots and facing round were attacking the Afghans with arrows from horseback in Turk fashion. One of these missiles killed Gujar Khan, and thereafter the Afghan vanguard melted away in a minute. Munim Khan himself returned to the field and completed the tally on his side.

At the other extremity, the Afghan left wing had attacked and somewhat shaken the imperial right division: Shaham Khan, the commander of the latter, himself "lost firmness on hearing of the boldness of Gujar and of the confusion of the imperial [central] army, and was turning back." [*Akbarnamah*, iii. 178]. But he was heartened by his braver subordinates, and this wing turned and fought the Afghans boldly. "In a short space of time the enemy [in front of them] was driven off and the victors proceeded against the (Afghan) centre." Threatened in front and left, with his vanguard dispersed beyond recall or sight, Daud could not maintain the contest long; his ruin was completed when news came of the fall of Gujar Khan and the flight of his division. The entire Afghan army now broke and fled in hopeless rout. The Mughals gave chase, slaying and plundering without opposition. "The plain became a tulip-garden from the blood of the slain."

Next day, the Mughal generalissimo, then in his 82nd year and suffering from senile decay (according to Abul Fazl), vented his wrath by killing all the prisoners taken and building eight towers with their heads. Daud fled to Katak, without being able to make a stand anywhere before the pursuing imperial army under Todar Mal. On 12th April he came out of that fort and made a complete submission.

CHAPTER XII

BATTLE OF HALDIGHAT, 1576

Babur's grandson, Akbar, who reigned over the empire of Delhi from 1556 to 1605, was the greatest ruler of India after Asoka, a born general and administrative organiser, a far-sighted statesman and a noble-hearted humanitarian. His aim was to make India strong by uniting all its parts under one sceptre and one reformed system of government. He, therefore, came up against the numberless petty chieftains of this continent of a country, who cherished their local independence above everything else. But Akbar won most of them over by his generous policy and crushed the others. The Rana of Mewar, the head of the Sisodia clan and the highest in honour among the Rajput tribes, refused to become Akbar's vassal. But the Emperor captured his capital Chitor after a memorable and bloody siege (1568) and occupied the eastern and more fertile half of his kingdom. Against the Rana, the Emperor sent Man Singh, heir to the Kachhwa house of Amber (later Jaipur) whose family had a hereditary feud with the Ranas of Mewar for past violations of territory. This Kachhwa family had recently risen to the highest rank and power by entering the Mughal service and displaying exceptional capacity for war and government under the Crown.

The Rana, Pratap Singh, took refuge in the western hills and forests of his dominion, in the rock-fortress of Kumbhalgarh (also called Kamalmer) and made his base at Gogunda (2757 feet above sea level), a town 16 miles north-west of Udaipur. It was necessary for Akbar to drive the Rana out of this post, in order to secure an easy route for the conquest of Gujrat from his own province of Malwa.

Man Singh, after calling in the Mughal detachments and mobilising his army at his base *Mandalgarh* (in Eastern Mewar), marched by way of *Mohi* (south of Raj-samund Lake) to the large village of Khamnor, south of the Banas river,

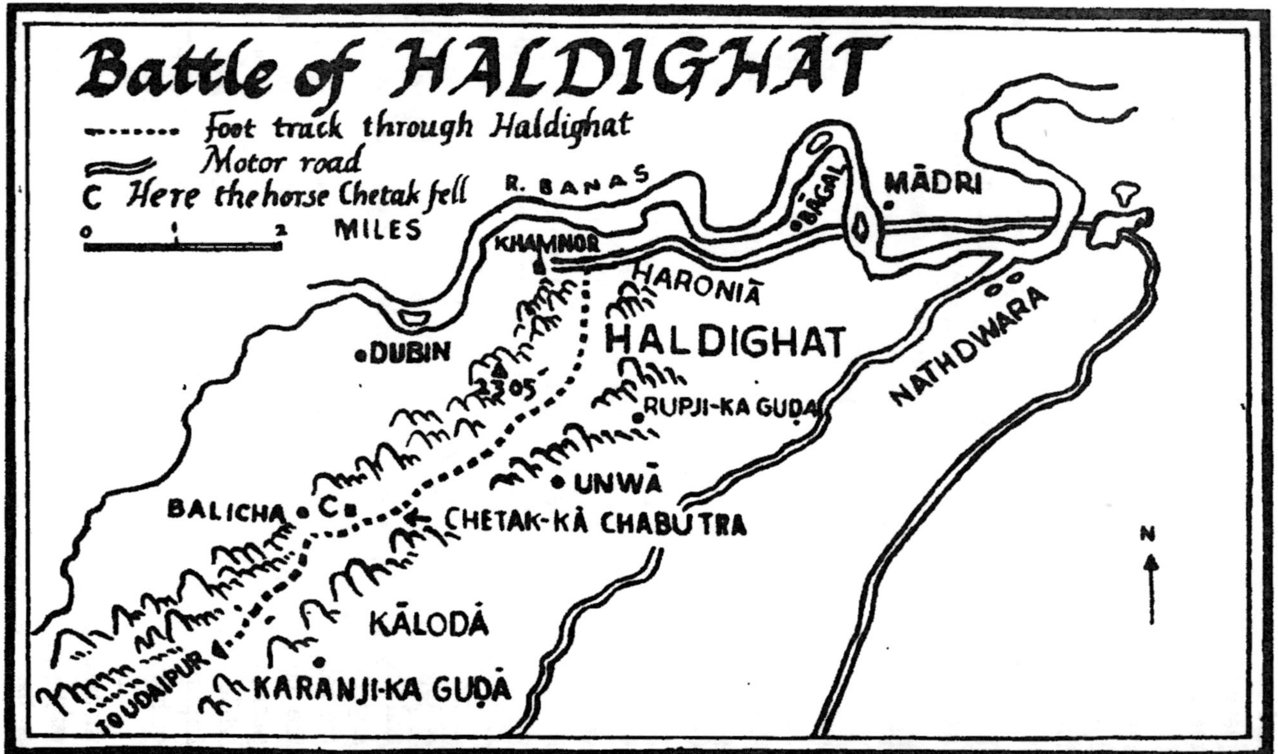
Battle of HALDIGHAT
Foot track through Haldighat
Motor road
C Here the horse Chetak fell
0
1
2
MILES
R. BANAS
KHAMNOR
HARONIĀ
HALDIGHAT
BĀGAL
MĀDRI
NATHDWARA
DUBIN
2305
RUPJI-KA GUḌA
UNWĀ
BALICHA
C
CHETAK-KĀ CHABUTRA
KĀLODĀ
KARANJI-KA GUḌĀ
TO UDAIPUR
N

and seven miles west of the famous temple of Nathdwara. This place is only 14 miles north of Gogunda, being separated from the latter by a spur of the Aravali chain, called the *Haldighat*, because its rock when crushed yields a bright yellow sand looking exactly like the turmeric (*haldi*) powder with which Indians spice their dishes. The Rana met the threat by advancing towards Khamnor and delivering battle on 18th June, 1576.

Rival Armies

The Rana's army is estimated by the eye-witness Al Badayuni at about (*bamiqdar*) three thousand horsemen, without any mention of infantry. The only foot-soldiers on his side were the Bhil bowmen of Punja (the chieftain of Merpur) who stood in the rear of the Rajput troopers, like the Pindharis behind the regular Maratha cavalry. Their number did not probably exceed 400, and they had no influence on the combat, because Bhils are not used to fighting pitched battles on open plains, but always ply their arrows from the cover of trees and rocks, and that day the Mughal army did not penetrate into the hills, so that the Bhils had no occasion to draw their bows.

It would be as fair a guess as we can make today to take Man Singh's total command as about ten thousand men. Out of these, some four thousand were his own clansmen (Kachhwas of Jaipur), one thousand (or less) were other Hindu auxiliaries, and five thousand (or a little more) Muslim troops of the imperial service. This proportion is a reasonable inference from the relative numbers of the officers of different races named in the contemporary Persian histories of the battle. Each side possessed elephants of war, but the Rajputs had no fire-arms, while the Muslims used a certain number of muskets of the improved pattern introduced by Akbar but no wheeled artillery or heavy ordnance (mortar).

The current Mewari tradition gives Man Singh *eighty* thousand men and the Rana *twenty* thousand out of whom only eight thousand survived. The proportion of four to one is the only thing correct here. These inflated figures are of a piece with the story that Pratap's horse Chetak jumped upon

Man Singh's elephant as a tiger climbs up a hunter's elephant and that one of its legs was cut off, after which it hobbled on three legs for two miles carrying its heavily armour-clad master on its back, till it fell down dead. Is not this a copy of *Chevy Chace*:—

For Witherington needs must I wayle,
As one in doleful dumpes;
For when his legs were smitten off,
He fought upon his stumpes.

The imperial army was thus marshalled: In the front rode a line of skirmishers, some 85 chosen heroes, led by Sayyid Hashim of Barha. Then came the Vanguard of brigaded Rajputs and Mughals, the Kachhwas under Jagannath and the Central Asian Mughals under Bakhshi Ali Asaf Khan (a Khawaja of Kazvin), a strong *iltmish* (advanced reserve) under Madho Singh Kachhwa, the Centre under Man Singh himself, and the Left Wing under Mulla Qazi Khan (later surnamed Ghazi Khan) of Badakhshan and Rao Lonkarn, the baron of Sambhar, with a band of the Shaikhzadas of Fathepur-Sikri (kinsmen of the saint Shaikh Salim Chishti). The strongest point in their line—in fact the pivot on which the imperial army turned—was the Right Wing, composed of the Sayyids of Barha, famous for their hereditary valour, which gave them the right to stand in the most dangerous and honourable position, at the right hand of the generalissimo. The Rear was formed by Mihtar Khan, at first at a great distance behind the front. Leaving out the Indian Muslims of Barha and Fathepur, the imperial troops were all crack horsemen and archers, from Central Asia, Uzbaks, Badakhshis, Quazzaqs and other tribes.

The Rana's Vanguard (about 800 horsemen), was commanded by Hakim Khan Sur (with his Afghan brethren), Bhim Singh, the baron of Dodia, Ramdas Rathor (a son of Jaimal, the martyred defender of Chitor), one Chundaot baron and some others. His Right Wing (say, 500 strong) was led by Ram Sah Tonwar, the dispossessed Rajah of Gwalior, with his three gallant sons and Bhama Shah, the Minister, with his brother Tarachand. In the Left Wing (say, 400 strong) were

Bida Mana and other Jhala clansmen. Pratap himself commanded the Centre (some 1,300 strong) mounted on his famous charger Chetak. In the Rear stood the Bhil bowmen of Punja, preceded by a group of bards (*charan*), priests (*purohit*), traders (*mahta*) and others usually counted as civilians, but who fought and bled like the best soldiers by caste.

In locating the actual site of the combat we are helped by some fixed points supplied by Al Badayuni: (1) The Mughal left wing was posted at the mouth of the pass (*dahna-i-ghati*), which was south-east of Khamnor, and therefore the imperial battle line stretched westwards from this point to a bend in the Banas river. (2) The Rana came into the field from behind the defile (*az 'aqb-i-dera*), and therefore he had passed the preceding night east of the range (at Lohsing according to the Mewari accounts). (3) The Rana's Vanguard under Hakim Khan Sur began the battle after debouching from the west side of the hill (*qiblaruia-i-Koh*). Therefore, the first clash of arms took place north-west of the Haldi range and not south-east of it. (4) The division under Pratap himself issued from the waist of the pass (*az-mian-i-ghati*) after Hakim Sur, and formed its wings in the plain.

When I visited Haldighat in October, 1934, my guide from Khamnor told me that the Rajput dead were washed and *cremated* at the now dried up tank called Rakt-ka-Tal, which was really their *smashan* and not the place where they had fought and fallen.

Tactics

Rana Pratap Singh staked his all on a desperate frontal charge, he kept no disposable reserve nor rear guard, for any emergency. Indeed, his total strength (only one-third of the Mughal numbers) was too small to permit him such a measure of precaution without greatly weakening his two attacking columns and taking the momentum out of his attack. Hence, his initial success could not be followed up, nor his check in the second stage ridden down. In fact, he followed what Captain Liddel Hart has called, "the wild-boar rush of Marshal Petain" in the First World War.

When the fighting became general, Raja Ram Sah Tonwar swerved from his original position in the right, where he had no work after the flight of his opposite number, the commander of the imperial left wing, and always pressed into the field in front of Pratap Singh, thus shielding the Rana's person, till he was slain by Jagannath Kachhwa. After the Mughal Vanguard and Left Wing had been scattered and their Right pressed hard, the main battle raged in the Centre. Here the Kachhwas of Amber grappled with the Sisodias of Mewar with the indescribable bitterness and fury which civil war between men of the same race usually breeds; challenges and taunts were hurled from one side to the other, and their captains had again and again to dash to the front and fight single-combats, the battle line swaying to and fro with every such movement.

During this second stage of the battle, the Muslim cavalry hovered round the ring, shooting their arrows and bullets with unerring effect into the mingled crowd of contending Rajputs in the centre, and cynically remarking. "On whichever side a man falls, it is a gain to Islam because it is one Hindu the less." (General Ali Asaf Khan's assurance to Al Badayuni).

The Rana's last resource was his war-elephants, and when these were overcome by the shooting off of their drivers, and the Mughal pressure on three sides began to drain the life blood of the Sisodias, striking down all their leaders one after another and finally the wounded Pratap Singh had to be led out of the field, the end came.

It was three hours after sunrise on the 18th of June, when the two armies first clashed together. From the western mouth of the pass issued a raging torrent of Afghans under Hakim Khan Sur and Rajputs under Ramdas, the son of Jaimal. The Afghans attacked with the burning rage of exiles against the usurpers of their homes. The impetuosity of this charge swept away the Mughal front line of skirmishers (only 85 men) in a twinkle and rolled them up upon the vanguard which itself was shaken and forced to give ground. Owing to the broken ground, jungle and crooked foot-tracks here, the Mughal cavaliers were huddled together in confusion, unable to deploy and counter-attack.

At the same time the imperial Left Wing was broken by

the attack of Raja Ram Sah and Bhama Shah; their opponents, Shaikhzadas of Sikri and Lon Karn's corps fled away "like a flock of sheep" from their post and passing by the Vanguard took refuge in their Right Wing. Both Qazi Khan and the Shaikhzada captain were wounded. The Right Wing itself was furiously attacked by Bida Jhala, but here the obstinate valour of the Sayyids of Barha upheld the imperial cause inspite of heavy slaughter by the Jhalas. This firm stand was rewarded; Man Singh's advanced reserve under Madho Singh galloped up to reinforce the hard-pressed Vanguard, which was also strengthened by the coming of Qazi Khan from the Left Wing and Sayyid Hashim from the front with a few staunch followers who had refused to flee. The battle line was thus stabilised and the fighting now became general.

By this time the two Centres were engaged, Rana Pratap and Man Singh each pressing forward with his men. The momentum of the Sisodia onset had been spent and the rival hosts were now locked together in a death embrace, and hand to hand fighting raged all over the field. "The warriors on both sides yielded up their lives but preserved their honour," as Akbar's Court historian admits: The Dodia baron, Bhim Singh, forced his way up to Man Singh's elephant and challenged him with the shout, "I am Dodia Bhim Singh, Come on, if you dare." He paid the price of his loyalty with his life.

Elephant Combats

The deadlock could be removed only by employing four-footed artillery. The Maharana sent his famous elephant "the rank-breaking *Lona*" to clear a path. Man and horse quailed before it. But the imperialists countered the move by driving forward their own "Pearl among elephants" (*Gajmukta*) to oppose it. "The shock of these two mountain-like forms threw the soldiers into trepidation, and the imperial elephant was wounded and about to fly when... a bullet struck the driver of the enemy's elephant and he turned back. But just then Pratap Tonwar brought forward *Ram Prasad*, which was the head of their elephants, and threw down many gallant men." At this time of wavering, two of the Mughal elephants, *Gajraj* and *Ran-madar,* were brought up to oppose Ram Prasad. But the driver of Ram Prasad was hit by an arrow in a vital place and thrown down to the ground by the shock of the charge. Then Husain Khan, the faujdar of the imperial elephants, with the greatest agility leapt from his own elephant on to the back of Ram Prasad and made prize that noted elephant, which had often been praised in Akbar's Court.

The hand-to-hand combat was now resumed. Kachhwa fought Sisodia in deadly rivalry. Ram Sah Tonwar (the ex-king of Gwalior) with his three gallant sons, who always kept in front of the Rana, "performed such prodigies of valour against the Rajputs of Man Singh as baffle description. Similarly, the young heroes who acted as the bodyguard of Man Singh performed such exploits as were a perfect model." This is the grudging testimony extorted from the bigoted Al Badayuni, an actor in this fight. In the heat of their onsets, the two supreme commanders once approached each other, but happily never came within reach of their spears. The Maharana was mostly opposed to Madho Singh Kachhwa, who led the all-important reserve. "Showers of arrows poured on the Rana who was wounded" by arrow and spear.

It was now mid-day. The contest had raged obstinately for three hours, and the Sisodias who had been under arms and moving for six hours, began to faint from the intense heat of mid-summer in that treeless plain shut round by hills. There were woeful losses on their side; Ramdas Rathor met with his father's heroic end by falling on the field. Ram Sah of Gwalior with his three sons—Salivahan, Bahan and Pratap Tonwar—perished "after showing extreme obstinacy of resistance, and there was none left to be his successor." (Al Badayuni). There were many others among the noble slain, of lesser note but no less valour than these.

The Final Scene

One act of the purest Rajput devotion was to light up the closing scene of Haldighat. By this time the tide of battle had turned irretrievably against the Maharana: his wings had been crumpled up and crowded upon his centre, which was hemmed round on three sides by the exultant imperialists. In the confusion the hope of Mewar himself was all but surrounded by the enemy and about to be cut off. But it was not to be, so long as there remained a single Rajput true to his chieftain. Realising the crisis, Bida, the Jhala baron, promptly snatched away the royal umbrella from over the head of Pratap Singh and rushed forward with it shouting that he himself was the Maharana and defying the imperialists to face him. The ruse succeeded; the Mughal captains, each eager to win the honour of being the Maharana's captor, crowded round Bida. The pressure on Pratap Singh was released, and his faithful adherents seizing his bridle turned his horse's head and led their wounded chieftain out of safety through the pass in their rear. Bida met with the death he had coveted. With his fall the struggle ended; the remnant of the Mewar army dissolved and fled through the pass or up the hillside, leaving 350 of their number to consecrate with their life blood the Thermopylae of Rajasthan. On the generally accepted calculation that the wounded are three times as many as the slain, the Mewar army that day endured casualties to the extent of 46 per cent of its total strength. From this we can judge of the fury of the fight. The imperialists lost about 150 slain and 350 wounded.

The Result

In the end, Haldighat proved a barren victory. No doubt the Mughals occupied Gogunda, but they could not oust the Rana from his north-western hills (Kumbhalgarh and Deosuri), nor could they occupy Gogunda long for want of provisions, the hostility of the population and the insecurity of the roads. As soon as the Mughal army of occupation withdrew, the Maharana came out of hiding and re-occupied the western part of his kingdom, while Chitor and eastern Mewar remained in Mughal hands. This uneasy state continued till after the death of both Akbar and Pratap Singh, when Jahangir granted an honourable peace to Pratap's son and successor, Amar Singh.

Chapter XIII

THE LAST MUGHAL-PATHAN BATTLE

Daulambapur, 1612

This is in many ways the most interesting Indian battle of the days before the English. For one thing, we have information about the strategic movements leading up to it and the equipment, tactics and actual course of the battle, with a minuteness of detail and accuracy of observation which are unequalled by any other of our battles before or after it. The report was written by a high military officer who fought in it and his record has been preserved ungarbled since then in a unique Persian manuscript.[1]

Daud, the last Karrani Sultan of Bengal, after his defeat by Akbar at Tukaroi (1575) made his submission, but rose again and was killed near Rajmahal (July 10, 1576). One of his ministers named Qutlu Lohani (Mian Khel) built up a small principality for himself in North Orissa by expelling Akbar's officers. When he died (in 1590), his followers, then led by his nephew Khawajah Usman Lohani were defeated by the imperial viceroy, Rajah Man Singh, exiled from Orissa and settled in the Khulna district on the South Bengal coast. Here they raised trouble, but were forced to migrate to the Dacca side of the great river, where Usman founded a new capital at Bokainagar in North Mymensingh. The Mughal pressure continued, and Usman, after losing Bokainagar, trekked further north with his followers and took shelter in South Sylhet, with his new seat at Patan Ushar (in

[1] *Baharistan-i-Ghaibi* (author Mirza Nathan, Shitab Khan), in the Biblio, Nationale of Paris, First English summary published by me in *J.B.O.R. Society* 1921; a full Bengali account of the battle by me in the *Prabasi* magazine (Agrahayan, 1328). Full English translation by Prof. M. I. Borah, *Baharistan-i-Ghyabi*, 2 Vols. (Govt. of Assam, 1938),—dangerously incorrect at places, (*e.g.*, i. 174, he translates that Usman had planted only one big cannon in his front battery, while the text gives the plural number).

the modern Maulavi Bazar Sub-division). The other Afghan chiefs, long settled in that region, were his natural allies.

In 1612, Islam Khan, the energetic imperial governor of Bengal, launched a great plan for crushing Usman and putting an end to the Afghan menace from the Sylhet side. From Dacca he detached one strong column (under Shaikh Kamal) against Bayazid Karrani, the chieftain of the older Afghan settlers in Sylhet, who had taken Usman under his protection, in order to prevent him from coming to the aid of his ally. A second army division was despatched against Usman under Shujait Khan Chishti. It was made up of a large number of horse and foot, among whom were 500 choice cavalry of the Governor's personal contingent, 4,000 musketeers, and about 100 elephants, accompanied by the whole of the imperial fleet in the East Bengal waters and the naval contingent of a vassal zamindar, and the artillery,—which maintained easy connection with the base at Dacca.

Shujait Khan marched from Dacca to Sarail (7 miles north of Brahmanberia town), where he left the fleet behind. Thence the army marched along the Meghna river for about 34 miles north-eastwards to Taraf (in the hills of South Sylhet) and next arrived at Putia-juri (5 miles north of Taraf) on 2nd February, 1612. Here he received more reinforcements from Dacca, consisting of 1,000 cavalry and a large body of musketeers, besides provisions. After another march of some five miles he arrived near Daulambapur, where he contacted the enemy. I identify this place as a village one mile north of the large lake called Hail Haor, and about five miles south of the modern town of Maulavi-Bazar; Uhar lay 13 miles west of it.

Usman had come out of his capital and entrenched his camp here. The place was admirably suited to the Afghan type of defensive war and the Afghan genius for making the best use of the terrain. A long narrow bog protected his front from the Mughal camp, which lay two miles away. A grove of large and thick betel-nut trees stood on the border of the marsh, and the Afghans by tying planks to these trees, formed a machan or raised battery on which large guns were mounted.

On 12th March, 1612, the Imperial army advanced from

its camp towards the marsh, in this order of battle:—The Vanguard was under Mirza Nathan (later surnamed Shitab Khan), the Right Wing under Iftikhar Khan, the Left under Kishwar Khan, the Centre under Shujait Khan himself and Ihtimam Khan, the Admiral, and the Advanced Reserve under Shaikh Qasim (the son of Shujait) with orders to support the Vanguard at need. All the big artillery was left behind in the camp and only a number of light pieces were carried along by the Vanguard, slung from poles borne by boatmen or mounted on the backs of elephants (swivels).

Usman's strength is computed by Nathan as 5,200 horsemen, 10,000 infantry and 140 elephants (from which figures we must make some deduction for inflation). He himself commanded the Centre, his brother Wali the Left, and his favourite slave Sher-i-Maidan the Right Wings, and two other brothers and a nephew his Vanguard. Usman's plan was to turn his camp into a fort with the long marsh before it as the ditch and the line of betel-nut trees on the water's edge as the rampart, with guns mounted on raised batteries of planks. These guns were trained on the known fords over the creek and under cover of their fire the Afghans could safely cross the water and attack the Mughals, while the imperial troops trying to reach the Afghan camp would be destroyed in the course of wading through that place in column formation. Inside this vast camp tents were pitched, groves arranged for sheltering and concealing the war-elephants, and food and munitions stored for the army. Hillocks and jungles guarded his two flanks against any turning movement from a distance.

The Afghans had so successfully camouflaged their camp that the Mughal army had no knowledge of their enemy's battle line. As the imperialists approached the scene, Murad Beg Aimaq (a Central Asian horse-archer leading the front scouts), on sighting the group of Afghans near the betel-nut grove, pointed it out as the enemy's main position. (But it was really their Left Wing). Immediately a wave of tumult passed through the imperial Vanguard, their pre-arranged plan of combat was thrown to the winds and a confused fighting began. The Van parted into three, one body swerving to the right in order to fight a party of Afghans who had boldly crossed the 'jhil' (marsh) near the betel-nut trees on to the Mughal side of the water. A second portion, without orders, hastened in the opposite direction and mingled with the front lines of their Left Wing, creating uncalled-for disorder there. But the main body of the Vanguard remained steady under its commander Mirza Nathan, who, however, could not fire his light guns planted in the ground and loaded. because of the mingled crowd of friends and foes before him.

To make matters worse for the Mughals, their big guns at position in the trenches two miles behind, now opened fire, hitting their own men in the front line from behind. Thus Shaikh Achha was killed and two other officers of the Right of the Van who had been engaged with the Afghan assailants were forced to retreat. For a time the close fighting ceased between the two Vanguards in the centre, who stood facing each other across the creek.

At the very opening of the battle, a disaster was brought down upon the imperial Right Wing by the indiscipline of its commander and the cowardice of its regular cavalry. Iftikhar Khan, proud of holding the most honourable post in the royal army, at the right hand of the commander-in-chief, had vowed to strike the first blow and deny that glory to the Vanguard. Therefore, as soon as the cry arose, "Our Van is advancing", he darted out of his own post at the core of the Right Wing, with 12 select heroes before him, 30 of his own troopers around and 14 devoted servants behind. Crossing the 'jhil' at his extreme right, by an obscure and unguarded ford which his local Muslim servant had spied out before, he reached the opposite bank in safety and fell on the Afghan Left Wing (commanded by Usman's brother Wali) like tigers. Though the rest of Iftikhar's command held back in cowardice, he and his 56 followers convulsed this Afghan Wing by their reckless fury. Wali gave ground and was about to flee, when Usman saw the danger and hastened to the spot with 2,000 horsemen and famous elephants, rescued his brother and enveloped the handful of Mughals. A most stubborn and cruel fight raged here. A powerful elephant of this Mughal wing was brought up across the 'jhil' to support Iftikhar, but it was at last 'made mince-meat of' by the crowd of Afghan horse and foot fighting on their own ground. Iftikhar himself was killed and his small band of heroic comrades annihilated. The contest on the Afghan side of the 'jhil' ended.

But the struggle had not been in vain; it had a decisive effect on the battle. One of the servants of Iftikhar sacrificed himself to avenge his master. Pressing close to Usman he gave him a mortal wound with his arrow, but paid the price of his daring with his own life. (Later, in the afternoon, Iftikhar's body was carried back by seven of his devoted retainers, three of whom fell in the attempt.)

All this time a severe battle had been raging at the opposite end of the Mughal line. Sher-i-Maidan, the commander of Usman's Right Wing, crossed the 'jhil' by a ford before him and fell upon the imperial Left Wing (under Kishwar Khan), driving away like chaff those men of the Mughal Vanguard who had rushed into its front only to create confusion. With unchecked momentum he next penetrated to the centre of this Wing where the General Kishwar Khan was slain "owing to the weakness and cowardice of his soldiers." The imperialists of this wing took to flight, and were chased up to their base camp. Turning back to the battle-field before the 'jhil', Sher-i-Maidan attacked the rear of the imperial Van from its left side. "A great confusion arose." But Mirza Nathan made such a bold stand that the exhausted Afghan horsemen of Sher-i-Maidan at last fled away to their own side.

But soon afterwards, the fighting was resumed in a more extensive and obstinate form. Usman's son Mumriz now arrived on the field with a vast force by the same route as Sher-i-Maidan (at the extreme right of the Afghan army). His famous war-elephants, the pride of Bengal, on being driven in front, at first caused havoc among the Mughal ranks. But the best elephants of the imperial army were brought up to counter these beasts, and a battle of indescribable confusion and ferocity raged all over the field,—the Mughals now huddled together, now scattering to avoid the path of the rushing mountains. The soldiers of the two sides were mingled together; brave captains challenged each other and fought single combats, and the famous elephants of the two sides were similarly matched against each other. On the whole, the

Bengal elephants proved their mastery and there were severe losses on the imperial side, most of the higher officers being killed or wounded.

"As the cavalry was engaged with the cavalry, the infantry with the infantry, and elephants with elephants, none could come to the help of others.... In short, from early morning till midday, hand to hand fighting was carried on." But in the course of time the mounted archery and elephant-borne swivel guns on the Mughal side, turned the tide in their favour. Many of the Afghan elephants were killed or disabled, their drivers shot off and the concentration of their cavalry broken up. At last, "when the Afghans found that the imperialists would not yield their ground, they became very much disappointed and took to flight," closely pursued by the Mughals up to the water's edge.

Thereafter a desultory fight continued till the afternoon. It was not known to the imperial army whether Usman was alive or dead, because his sons carried on the war undismayed by his death. "The warriors on both sides were extremely tired of this hard fought battle and had lost the power of rushing forward. Arrows, bullets and cannon-balls were kept showering from both sides," but the better artillery and marksmanship of the Mughals got the better of the enemy.

The hand to hand fighting had ceased by midday; the exchange of fire across the 'jhil' continued till midnight when it died out on the Afghan side. Some six hours before dawn, the Afghans secretly evacuated their camp, carrying away all their elephants, artillery and infantry as well as the corpse of their chieftain. Then only did the Mughals learn that the victory was theirs.

In this battle, two principles of war are well illustrated; First, that other things being tolerably well matched, the character of the general decides the issue of the fight. Secondly, the fully equipped "regular" Mughal army with its heavy cavalry and guns is reduced to impotence in the swamps and jungle of East Bengal, if the opposite side can make a clever use of the terrain and its advantages for the defence. The Bengal Afghans fought this battle with inferior numbers, poorer equipment and inadequate munitions. Their soldiers were mostly East Bengal rustics many of whom had only recently changed their bamboo rods for sword and shield. The loss of their contact with Chittagong and Noakhali had robbed them of the means of increasing their fire-arms and gun powder by purchase from the Portuguese; and their horses were sorry country ponies. And yet the genius of their leader Khwaja Usman and the fighting spirit of their race almost caused a disastrous defeat of the superior force of the imperialists.

At Daulambapur the uneven and marshy ground, no doubt, proved a handicap to the imperial cavalry who could not follow their usual tactics suited to dry open plains. The disorder was made worse by their war elephants getting out of control, and thus impeding cavalry action. But when everything has been said, the fact cannot be denied that Shujait Khan failed in a General's duty to hold his divisions strictly together and control the battle, with the result that each wing commander acted as he liked or was forced to act. If his four thousand foot musketeers had been tactically employed, they alone could have neutralised twice the number of Afghan horsemen.

The memoirs of Mirza Nathan illustrate the notorious jealousy raging among the imperial officers in Bengal (notably between the General and the Admiral). The Mughal army was sick of campaigning in the unhealthy climate of East Bengal and had no heart in its work. During this battle the foot musketeers (Hindus of Bihar) rebuked the Mughal cavalry (Central Asians) for holding back and deserting their captain.

The most memorable fact of this battle was the bold front presented by the Indo-Afghans and their continued fighting for the whole day, after their chief had fallen in the forenoon. They even kept Usman's death a secret from their enemy till next morning. Thus they succeeded in keeping their camp unviolated by the enemy till they could fully evacuate it under cover of the night. This was an astonishing performance for an Asiatic army.

CHAPTER XIV

TALIKOTA, Jan. 5, 1565

Talikota is rightly called the most decisive battle of South India. It effected a revolutionary change in the history of the entire Deccan. It shattered the great Vijaynagar empire into fragments, turned that splendid capital into a desolate wilderness, and left the Hindus of southern India so disunited and crushed that they could never again raise their heads in full sovereignty.

To the military student this battle is of interest as repeating the story of Alexander's victory over Porus in its essential features, though differing in some particulars, such as the use of artillery and elephants on both sides. Here we have again the sure triumph of a choice cavalry force over a multitude of ill-armed rustic infantry. Here again true generalship overcame a fourfold superiority in mere numbers, though the arms were of the same kind on both the sides.

The Rival Armies Contrasted

The crushing defeat of Vijaynagar was the natural effect of the Hindu armies neglecting the cavalry arm and long range missile weapons, and their leaders riding on elephants instead of swift horses of the best breed. The Hindu infantry was strong only in number, mustering hundreds of thousands, but they formed a neglected arm; the men were without armour or even coats; their bodies were naked except for a loin cloth and a turban, and their weapons were the Indian bow, made of bamboo, which could send an arrow only a short distance. Their cavalry numbered (on the average) about one-twentieth of their infantry and they were mostly mounted on countrybred ponies, unable to bear the weight of armour or lend momentum to a charge. Their horsemen plied the sword and the short spear (only six feet long), so that they could hit the enemy only when they came close enough to fight hand to hand.

The Vijaynagar army had a branch of firearms, consisting of large pieces of ordnance, rockets and muskets, but except for the rockets (which acted rather like playthings), this department was manned entirely by foreigners,—Portuguese half-castes and black Christians from Goa. The famous *Kalapiadas* or Karnataki foot musketeers, recruited from the Berad and other wild tribes, came into being a century later. The artillery of Vijaynagar was antiquated and cumbrous when compared with the improved and modernised firearms of the Sultans of the Deccan who frequently corresponded with their brother Shias of Persia and through the Persian Gulf with Turkey (the best-armed Muslim Power in the world). W. Haig speaks of "Nizam Shah's wonderful train of 700 guns."

The foreign cavalry of the Deccani Sultans' armies were mounted on powerful horses of the Arab breed, purchased through the Portuguese by way of Chaul and Goa. We read that a few years before this battle, Adil Shah of Bijapur had bought up all the Arab horses imported for sale at the port of Goa. The Vijaynagar Emperors formerly used to buy every year 13,000 horses of Ormuz and country-breds at the western ports, but that practice had been abandoned during Ram Raja's regency of 40 years.

Moreover, the Muslim troopers coming from Iran and Turan were fully armour-clad and plied the terribly effective composite bow (made of steel or two horns joined together with a metal clasp) which shot arrows with a longer range and greater penetrating power than the bamboo bows of the Hindus. This Muslim cavalry force was also stiffened by a certain proportion of men carrying long lances (16 feet) and javelins of metal which could reach riders on elephants, and easily push back opponents seeking hand to hand combats with swords and short spears.

Ram Raja had formed a corps of Muslim cavalry by enlisting six Muslim mercenary captains who had left the service of the Deccan Sultans with their retainers. He had cherished them well, but they were Indo-Muslims, men of a lower type of intelligence and martial skill than the newly arrived foreign mounted archers of Iran and Turan who formed the backbone of the Sultans' armies. In fact, they were Indian Pathans or Ruhelas whom we find a century later dominating the army of Adil Shah.

Why the Hindus were Defeated

The contrast in the opposed generalship was still greater than that in equipment or arms. On the allied side there was the towering genius of Ikhlas Khan of Ahmadnagar, Kishwar Khan of Bijapur and Mustafa Khan of Golkonda, and the matchless skill of Chelebi Rumi Khan, Nizam Shah's artillery chief, the whole confederacy was welded together by the iron will and controlling power of Husain Nizam Shah. Hence, in this battle the tactical combination of heavy cavalry with artillery was perfectly timed and most effective.

On the Hindu side cohesion among the three divisions was lost as soon as the battle started. The Vijaynagar army depended solely on three aged generals,—Ram Raja over eighty and his brothers Tirumal and Venkatadri each above 60 years. They had not under them a group of dependable divisional brigadiers, capable of seizing the initiative or rallying the men with changes in the tide of battle. And thus, their supreme leader's fall meant the rout and destruction of the entire army; no orderly retreat, no defensive rearguard action, nor even a stand to protect the national capital could be attempted by the Hindus.

The lesson taught by this battle has been thus put by Lt.-Col. Sir Wolseley Haig:—"The victory of the Muslims against such overwhelming odds has the appearance of a miracle, but the superiority of their artillery and of their troops, especially the foreigners (i.e., Iranis and Turanis) helps to explain it. Their cavalry was better armed, better mounted, and excelled in horsemanship, and the mounted archers, of whom the Hindus seem to have had none remaining, were probably at least twice as efficient as cavalry equal to them in other respects, but armed only with sword or lance. The main strength of the Hindu army was its infantry, ill-armed, ill-clad, ill-trained, and deficient in martial spirits." (*Cambridge History of India*, iii. 450).

When the famous Bahmani empire of South India began

to decline, early in the 16th century, independent Sultanates were founded by its rebel officers at Ahmadnagar, Bijapur and Golkonda, besides two smaller ones. These three began to expand their territories at the expense of the Hindu empire of Vijaynagar, which stretched from sea to sea in their south. There were frequent wars between the two sides, the Raichur doab between the Tungabhadra and the Krishna rivers being the chief bone of contention, and many atrocities were committed by both sides in the course of these wars. At last in 1574 Husain Nizam Shah, the Sultan of Ahmadnagar, thirsting for revenge, formed an alliance with the Sultans of Bijapur (Ali Adil Shah I) and Golkonda (Ibrahim Qutb Shah) for a joint war to crush the power of Vijaynagar. The Barid Shahi Sultan of Bidar joined the Golkonda forces, but his contingent was too small to count.

Muslim Strategy: Krishna Crossed By Surprise

The armies of the three confederates assembled in the plain outside Bijapur, and after ten days of feasting and planning there, set out on 24th December, 1564, to invade Vijaynagar territory on the other side of the Krishna. They reached Talikota, a town on the eastern bank of the Don river, 48 miles south-east of Bijapur on the 27th. Next day marching southwestwards from Talikota they arrived at the north bank of the Krishna at Tangadgi, 24 miles from their last station and 9 miles south of the large town of Mudde Bihal. The best ferry over the river was here, four miles east of the village of Tangadgi and six miles below the point (Sangam) where the Malprabha falls into the Krishna.

But meantime, Ram Raja, the regent and *de facto* ruler of Vijaynagar, had arrived there and fortified the southern bank of their river with trenches and batteries of big guns which commanded the crossing. The army and material resources of his empire lay behind, to resist the Muslim invasion.

The Hindus were obsessed by the Maginot Line mentality and thought only of defence. They fortified their post and remained inactive within their own limits to see how things would turn up. The Muslim generals, on the contrary, show-

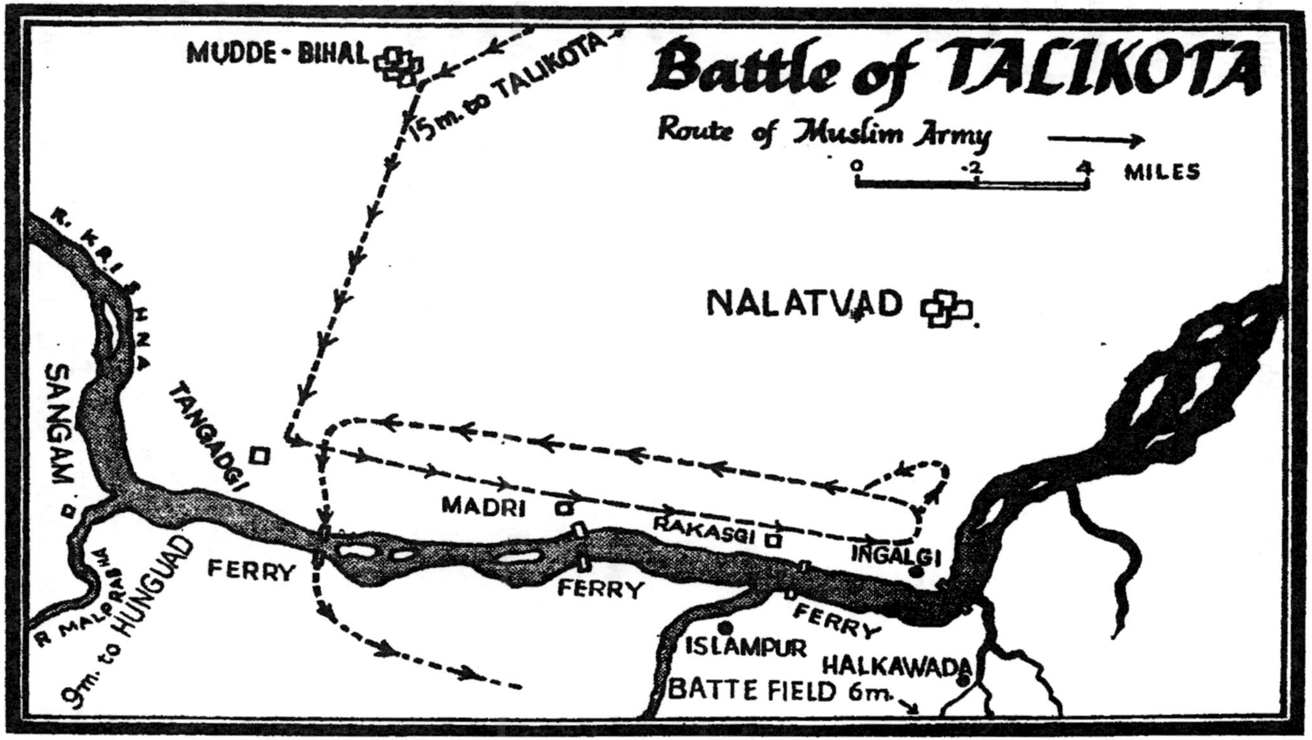

Battle of TALIKOTA
Route of Muslim Army
0 ·2 4 MILES
MUDDE - BIHAL
15m. to TALIKOTA
NALATVAD
R. KRISHNA
SANGAM
TANGADGI
MADRI
RAKASGI
INGALGI
FERRY
FERRY
FERRY
R MALPRABHA
9m. to HUNGUAD
ISLAMPUR
HALKAWADA
BATTE FIELD 6m.

ed a masterly spirit of enterprise and rapidity of action. By a stroke of strategic genius, they deceived the Hindus and "stole a crossing over the river" (as has been aptly put in a parallel case by a historian of Alexander's campaign against Porus). If the confederated Sultans had tried to force a crossing there, it would have only led to a useless massacre of their men; so they formed a subtle plan. Giving out that they would not cross the Krishna there, but go to an undefended third ferry further down the river, they marched eastwards along the north bank for two days in succession. On seeing this move of his enemy Ram Raja also marched parallel to them along the south bank withdrawing his guns and guards from the ferry opposite Tangadgi.

After two marches, the Muslimagenerals on the third day (2nd January, 1565) sent a small detachment to continue the advance in the same easterly direction, while a strong body of their cavalry turned back to make a forced march in the opposite direction to the first ferry. It was composed of picked men mounted on the fleetest and hardiest horses and led by Husain Nizam Shah, with mobile artillery (camel-swivels and elephant-borne pieces, called *gajnal*).

Being concealed from the eyes of the Hindu spies on the south bank by the dust and tumult raised by their brethren making the deceptive march, these horsemen reached the Tangadgi ferry in the course of twelve hours. There was none to oppose them there, only the silent abandoned trenches of Ram Raja on the opposite bank. Nizam Shah, without waiting for the rest of the army to join him, at once forded the Krishna, occupied in force both ends of the ferry, and sat astride the river. In the course of the next day (3rd Jan.) the rest of the Muslim army arrived and the men, guns and baggage were all safely transported to the southern bank.

No time was lost. The next day (4th January) the three Sultans, drawing up their troops in battle formation and leaving their camps behind, marched along the south bank, seeking the enemy out. Meantime, Ram Raja, astonished by his enemy's strategic victory over him, had turned back to meet them on the way. But, on coming in contact with them he refused battle on that day and fell back to his own camp, deciding to fight on the morrow. Thus the Muslim army gained full one day to rest and refresh themselves after four continued marches.

Location Of Battle-Field—Formation Of Troops On Two Sides

The encounter took place at noon, on Friday, 5th January, 1565, the second of Jamadi-us-Sani 972 A.H. at some distance (about 6 miles) south-east of the village of Rakasgi (which stands eight miles east of Tangadgi), and by joining the names of these two places we get the correct location of the field mis-called Talikota. Fifteen miles south of Talikota is the town of Nalatvad, and 6 miles further south stands the village of Ingalgi on the north bank of the Krishna, where the river after flowing east from Sangam takes a sharp bend to the north. After crossing the river here to the south bank, 14 miles further south-east stands the large city of Mudgal. A straight line connecting Ingalgi with Mudgal cuts through the battle-field. (Sewell, p. 200 *n* and Degree Sheet $\frac{56\text{ d}}{\text{sw}}$, scale 1 in. = 2 m.). The two armies were so vast that the actual scene of the contest must have occupied an area six miles in width and four miles in depth.[1]

The Muslim army was reported by a Portuguese writer to consist of 50,000 cavalry and 3,000 infantry. The last figure included the men who worked the guns, totalling 600 pieces from large ordnance to hand-guns. They had also a number of elephants, both champion-fighters and transport beasts. The spearhead of the Muslim attack was a select corps of Khurasani and Turkish horsemen about eight thousand strong.

The Hindu army is calculated by Indian writers at colossal

[1] Sewell hazards a guess that the Sultans crossed at Ingalgi. I disagree. I also follow the *Burhan-i-Maasir* (against Firishtah) in making Venkatadri the leader of the Hindu Right Wing and the antagonist of Qutb Shah, (p. 967 of my ms.). The original Persian texts of the *Burhan* and Firishtah have been used by me, rejecting Briggs's grossly incorrect trans. of the latter and King's condensed version of the former. *Tazkirat-ul-muluk* gives no detail of the campaign though its author saw desolate Vijaynagar only ten years after this battle.

figures which stagger the imagination, anything up to one million. A sober estimate would be 60,000 horsemen of all sorts, a host of hardy but ill-armed, ill-trained footmen just exceeding one lakh, and 1,000 elephants and some antique guns and hundreds of rockets. A corps of mercenary Muslim

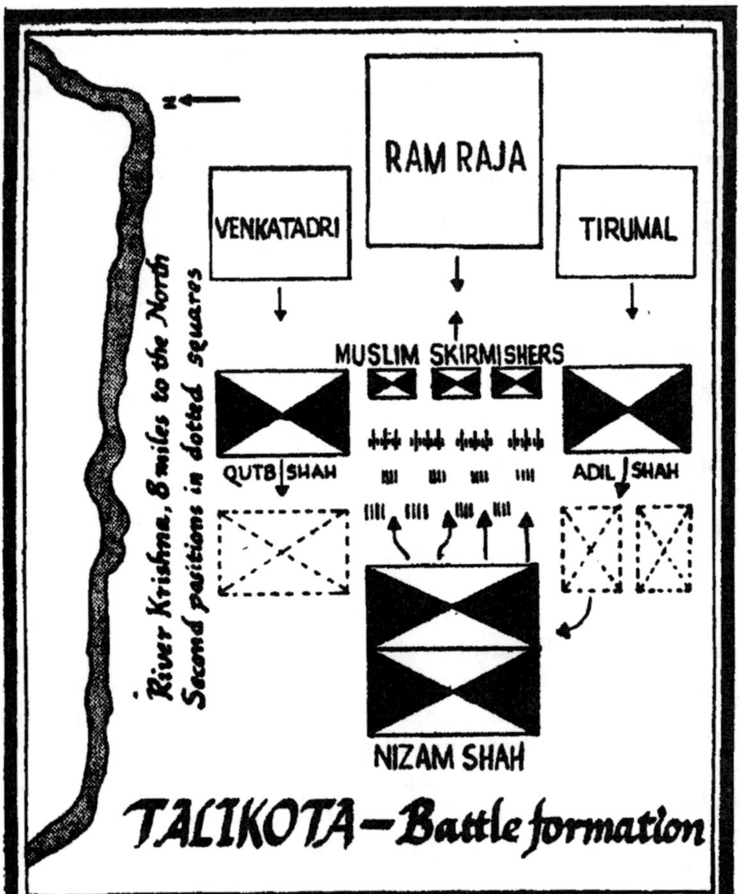

horse-archers, probably 2,000 in number and fairly well-mounted, were on this side. But the remaining troopers of Vijaynagar rode small country-breds and mares, every subject in the realm who possessed a horse having been summoned by Ram

Raja to join his banners; these men mostly fought with sword and short spear.

The confederated Muslim army was divided into its three national component parts,—the Golkonda troops under Ibrahim Qutb Shah and his general Mustafa Khan with the small Bidar quota formed the Left Wing; the Bijapuris under Ali Adil Shah I and his general Kishwar Khan Lari the Right Wing, while the Ahmadnagar force under Husain Nizam Shah and his general Ikhlas Khan formed the Centre with the powerful artillery train under Rumi Khan Chelebi planted in front. The guns were thus arranged: 200 big pieces of ordnance were taken out of their carts and planted in the first line, being joined together by chains and ropes, with spaces left at intervals to allow the passage of cavalry (exactly the tactics of Babur). Some distance behind them was the second line of 200 medium-sized guns (called *Zarb-zan*), and similarly behind these 200 smaller swivels (called *zamburak*) which were larger than hand-muskets. These were kept loaded and primed, and a screen of 2000 expert Turkish horse-archers was spread before the first line to deceive the Hindus and lure them unsuspecting up to the very muzzles of the big guns. The mass of their troops, all cavalry, with elephants were retired behind the guns.

Battle : First Stage

It was already noon when the battle began. After the invariable preliminary of big gun fire and rocket discharge, which did little harm, the two wings of the Vijaynagar army made an impetuous charge upon their respective opposites. The weakest part of each army faced its enemy at the northern end of the line. The Muslim Left Wing here was composed of the troops of Qutb Shah (and Barid Shah) who were ranked among the Deccani Muslims as the poorest in quality and their leadership almost contemptible. W. Haig calls Qutb Shah "a broken reed". They were attacked by Venkatadri, the least worthy of the three regent brothers of Vijaynagar; his conduct after this defeat showed him to be a selfish coward. He was not the man to exert himself to the utmost and "lose or gain it all." It is clear that when the tumultuous first assault of the Hindu Right Wing forced the Golkonda troops back, the victorious impetus was not continued, the enemy were not routed, but they rallied after retreating a short distance and then held the ground till the end. Thus they immobilised this Hindu Wing till all was over elsewhere.

At the southern end of the line, where Adil Shah was assailed by the Hindu Left Wing under Tirumal, the fighting was the most obstinate and bloody of the whole afternoon. Tirumal and his gallant son Raghunath fought on till they were severely wounded,—the father being blinded by an arrow and the son probably so wounded as to have to be carried away bleeding from the field. In fact, these two heroes pass out of history after this battle, which clearly means that they died soon after it. Here the Bijapuri defence was led by a spirited Persian general Kishwar Khan Lari, the veteran of many wars in India. The attack of Tirumal at first shook the Bijapuri cavalry and forced it to give some ground. But Kishwar Khan adopted the Cossack tactics of Central Asia; his horse-archers wheeled round in their flight and plied their arrows with deadly effect on the Hindu crowd following them in disorder. After full three hours of this ding-dong fighting, the Hindu Left Wing broke and fell back defeated. Ali Adil Shah seized the respite and without a moment's delay sent Kishwar Khan with his 5,000 foreign horse-archers to the Centre "with the speed of wind and lightning" to join Nizam Shah's cavalry in the last decisive charge of the day.

All this time, the Muslim Centre, their strongest division, had held. At first, following the Turkish tactics, a body of 2,000 horse-archers, called the *Qarawwal,* had been sent forward by Husain Nizam Shah to engage the Hindu Vanguard in front of Ram Raja's Centre. They were at once charged by the Hindus in a tumultuous body, and after some exchange of blows, fell back slowly. This was a trick of war, for, as they fled to their own side. the Hindus arrived at their heels in reckless pursuit, close to Nizam Shah's front line of guns. The cavalry screen withdrew to their own rear through the intervals left for the purpose between the guns, and Rumi Khan discharged his pieces among the swarming mass of the enemy, with murderous effect, and they fell back battered and torn.

Battle : Decisive Final Tactics

Thus after swaying to and fro for three hours, the battle went against Ram Raja all along his line. A pause in the combat followed. Ram Raja was too old and weak to mount horse or elephant (*Firishta*). So, he had been carried into the field in a sedan-chair (litter or *palki*). Nizam Shah at the height of the dubious combat had set up his special royal tent in front of his post, which proclaimed to the world that he would not leave the place without either victory or death. Ram Raja, on his side, planted a pavilion and sat down on a throne under it with heaps of money and jewels by his side, out of which he promptly gave handfuls to his men who fought well. Harangued by him, the brigadiers of his Centre rallied their men and led a second attack upon the Muslim Centre, in a huge mass, the rear ranks pushing the front lines forward.

For this manoeuvre the Ahmadnagar artillery chief was prepared and coolly waiting. As soon as the wild Hindu multitude came within point blank range he discharged his guns, loaded with bags full of thick slug-like copper coins instead of shot, and after this one salvo 5,000 Hindus lay dead and writhing in a human mound before the Muslim Centre. This "whiff of grape" finished the Hindus and their last venture was quenched in blood.

Seizing this psychological moment, a large and compact force of select Khurasani horsemen who had been carefully reserved for this last stroke, now issued through the intervals between the guns and forming line crashed into the crowd of the Hindu horse, foot and elephantry under Ram Raja's own command. Indescribable confusion and dust enveloped the field; no command could be heard or even issued, and the Turki cavalry (5,000 men under Kishwar Khan the Persian joined to 2,000 men of the same race in Nizam Shah's pay) pierced through the helpless leaderless enemy crowd without a check, with an elephant corps following close behind. All order was lost.

A wild elephant of Nizam Shah charged and overtook the sedan-chair into which Ram Raja had now entered to escape. His bearers dropped it in terror and fled away. He was taken prisoner by Chelebi Rumi Khan and brought to Hussain Nizam Shah who at once cut off his head and exposed it on the point of a lance to the view of all the field.

The leaderless Vijaynagar army broke in helpless rout. Venkatadri alone made a safe retreat to the capital with the utmost haste. The rest of that vast army continued to be massacred in pursuit till the early sunset of that winter evening put a stop to their slaughter. Tradition counted the Hindu dead as one lakh of men. But 16,000 slain and thrice that number wounded, would be as correct an estimate as it is possible for us to make. But the empire of Vijaynagar ceased to exist and its capital was turned into a howling wilderness.

CHAPTER XV

BATTLE OF BHATVADI

The battle of Bhatvadi is very famous in Maratha history. It no doubt raised Malik Ambar's fame and power to the highest pitch and surrounded his last years with a blaze of glory. But it was a mere skirmish with plan and concerted action only on the victor's side and disunion, cowardice and slackness on the part of his enemies, so that we can hardly dignify it with the name of a battle. We also know no precise detail about the course of the fighting. I reconstruct the story from the contemporary Persian history of Fuzuni (written in 1640) and Jahangir's *Autobiography* (1626). It has no lesson of strategy or tactics to illustrate, but only teaches us how a coalition should *not* conduct war.

Malik Ambar, an Abyssinian slave of extraordinary ability for war and administration alike, made himself the regent for the puppet Nizam Shahi Sultan of Ahmadnagar, after the capital of that State had been annexed by Akbar. At first victorious over the generals of Emperor Jahangir, and the Bijapur (Adil Shah) and Golkonda (Qutb Shah) forces, he was humbled by that Mughal Emperor's eldest son Shah Jahan and forced to restore all his conquests from the Mughals (1621). When Prince Parviz, the next Viceroy of Mughal Deccan, left for Delhi (1624), Adil Shah bribed him with 12 lakhs of rupees to detach the entire expeditionary force of the imperialists in the Deccan and their Maratha auxiliaries to help him in recovering the province of Bidar, which Ambar had conquered and an old Nizam-Shahi possession lately annexed by Adil Shah.

The mercenary Mughal generals accompanying the Bijapuri Wazir Mulla Muhammad Lari, set out from Malwa to invade Ahmadnagar territory. But Ambar, with marvellous energy for an old man of eighty first struck. Marching out, he exacted a heavy contribution from the Golkonda Sultan and then swiftly turned back to raid the environs of Bijapur city. But finding that now at last the hired Mughal contingent under Md. Lari from the north and a Bijapuri army under Ikhlas Khan from the east were converging upon him, he slipped back to his own kingdom and took shelter in the fort of Bhatvadi, about ten miles south-east by east of the fort of Ahmadnagar, and on the western bank of the Keli Nadi, a small feeder of the Sina river.

The three confederated armies, Mughal, Adil Shahi, and Qutb Shahi, came and sat down before Bhatvadi. There was no union of heart or of command among them. The only concern of the Delhi generals was to get as much money out of the Bijapuri Sultan and do as little work for him as possible; they were estranged, because he could not satisfy their greed fully after having paid 12 lakhs of rupees to their prince. Even the Bijapuri army formed a house divided against itself, as Ikhlas Khan, the commander of its Abyssinian section, was jealous of the Minister Mulla Md. Lari and constantly quarrelled with him. The Golkonda troops had no fighting value except against uncivilised petty jungle chieftains. Thus about two months passed in inaction.

Malik Ambar played a waiting game in his defence. By letting out the water of the Bhatvadi lake, he barred the path before the Mughal army; the excess of mud weakened his enemy, but though his men were fewer, his heart remained confident. The rainy season invested the ground with a mantle of water. Scarcity of food reached the extreme in the two besieging camps. For two or three nights together neither beast nor man got any food, till at last no strength for movement was left in their bodies. A large convoy of treasure and provisions sent by Adil Shah could not approach the camp for fear of Ambar's troops. Many soldiers and even officers, unable to bear the privation any longer, deserted to Ambar, and his good treatment of them encouraged more desertions from the besieging armies.

Soon Ambar's men began to make successful raids on the enemy posts at night. The invading troops were utterly demoralised and no captain would go out to bring provisions in. At last Mulla Md. Lari sent out a large detachment with all

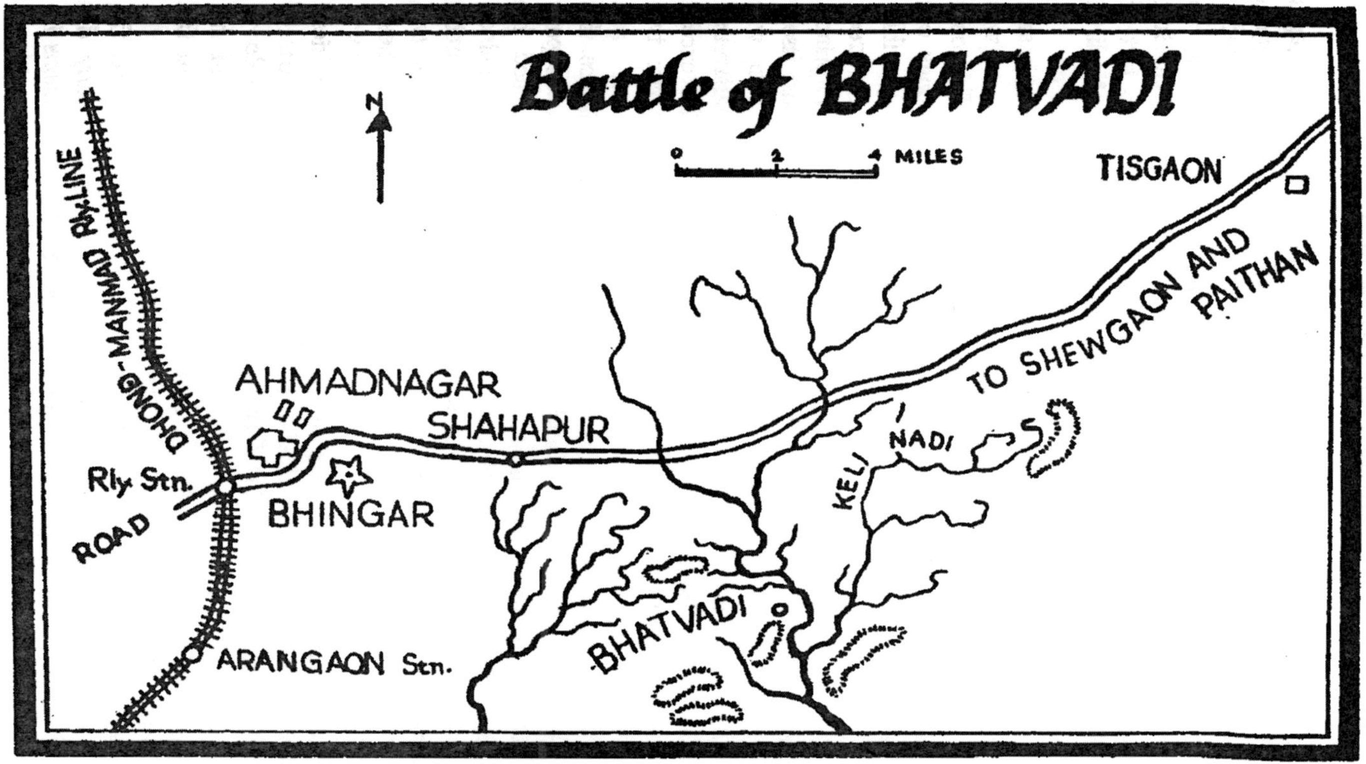

Battle of BHATVADI
N
0 2 4 MILES
TISGAON
TO SHEWGAON AND PAITHAN
DHOND-MANMAD Rly. LINE
AHMADNAGAR
SHAHAPUR
Rly. Stn.
ROAD
BHINGAR
ARANGAON Stn.
KELI NADI
BHATVADI

his best cavalry under Mustafa Khan to escort the treasure and provisions from Bijapur waiting at a distance, and thus fatally weakened himself for the day of combat.

With this growing increase in Ambar's numbers and the spirit of his captains and a corresponding decrease in his enemy's, his attacks became more frequent and more open. As the historian Fuzuni writes, "The Mughal army laboured under several difficulties from which Ambar's troops were free, namely, famine and hunger, disunion, two hearts, two languages, excess of rain. These ruined them."

On the fateful day, Mulla Md. Lari was urged by the imperial generals to join them in a desperate attempt to cut their way through the ring of the enemy and ride hard to their base at Ahmadnagar. When he came back to the Bijapuri army, he found their chief Ikhlas Khan in despair and proposing surrender to the enemy. But by this time the battle had already joined. The aged Minister found that his policy of war with Ambar by an alliance with the Mughals had utterly failed and he had nothing to show in return for the twelve lakhs of his master's money which he had spent in buying their barren aid. His Court rival Ikhlas Khan was exulting at his failure and blaming him for the ruin of their troops. So, in utter disgust with life, he left Ikhlas Khan and spurred his horse alone (with only three kinsmen following) towards Ambar's ranks and found the soldier's death that he coveted.

It happened in this way. In the morning the Delhi generals thinking that there would be no fighting that day, were passing their time in idleness and off their guard, when a force of Ambar's regular cavalry (Ambar's guard corps of Abyssinian youths) were sighted at a distance, looking as if they were retreating after breaking off an engagement. So the Mughals took no heed of them, nor got ready for self-defence. That body of cavalry, after skirting the Mughal detachment, suddenly turned round and fell on the Bijapuri troops and after a severe fight broke them. At that time Mulla Md. Lari was slain (by his Bijapuri rival's partisans from behind, according to one report) and the defeat of his side became a hopeless rout. The Marathas in Adil Shahi pay fled away without fighting.

It was a most complete victory achieved in an incredibly short time. Ikhlas Khan and 24 other leading commanders of Bijapur were taken prisoner, and among the imperial generals, three were captured, while the others "saved themselves from whirlpool" by hard riding to the Mughal frontier, abandoning everything in their camp.

I reject the statement of the poet Paramanand, a Maratha court flatterer, who wrote 54 years after this battle that Shahji Bhonsle took the leading and even the sole part, in fighting for Ambar and ensuring his victory. No contemporary and no Muslim authority mentions it. Fuzuni, writing in 1640, says that the cavalry of Ambar that delivered the attack were *Turkha* or Turks, technical name for foreign heavy cavalry, the exact opposite of the Maratha light horse.

CHAPTER XVI

WAR FOR THE DELHI THRONE
(1658-1659)

This war of succession among Shah Jahan's sons is an interesting subject for military students, because it was a civil war in which the troops, organisation and leaders were of the same race and education and both the sides were backed by the resources and prestige of a government,—a provincial government in the case of the rebels and the Central State in the case of the other side. The signal difference in the character of the rival generalship alone accounts for the glaring difference in the result, when the forces were nearly matched in numbers and equipment.

The Emperor Shah Jahan after a long and prosperous reign of 30 years fell very ill in September 1657. He had already completed 67 lunar years of age, and when his life was despaired of, his three younger sons, who were governors of provinces, prepared to contest the throne against their eldest brother Dara Shukoh, who was in attendance on their ailing father at the capital. Of these four princes, the ablest and most experienced by far was Aurangzib, then Governor of Mughal Deccan. He cleverly completed his preparations for war, but at the same time concealed his plans and deceived his two brothers, by not crowning himself but promising to help the other two who had crowned themselves,—Murad in Gujrat and Shuja in Bengal.

Leaving the Deccan at the head of a highly efficient and organised army and a band of very able officers, he crossed the Narmada at Akbarpur (3rd April, 1658) and entered Malwa, on the way to Delhi. Meantime Dara Shukoh, who had been declared heir to the throne by the invalid Emperor, had taken charge of the administration at the capital, without crowning himself. He sent three armies from there against his three rebellious brothers—under Mirza Raja Jai Singh against Shuja, under Qasim Khan against Murad, and under Maharaja Jaswant Singh against Aurangzib. The last two generals were to unite and oppose the two princes, if the latter formed a junction. Jaswant and Qasim Khan, in consequence of their slothful habits, lack of news service, and Qasim Khan's jealousy and faithlessness, failed to keep Murad and Aurangzib apart and the two princes united their forces at Dipalpur on the way (14th April). Thus the rebel strategy was successful and this was the first blow at the Government troops.

Contact at Dharmat

From Ujjain, the capital of the province of Malwa, Jaswant advanced 14 miles south-westwards to Dharmat, a village on the western bank of the Gambhira rivulet, and close to the modern railway junction Fatihabad-Chandravati. Aurangzib and Murad came up here and gave him battle on 15th April, 1658, the morning after their arrival.

The two armies were nearly matched, being about 35,000 men each, but Aurangzib was immensely superior in artillery, as he had taken over Mir Jumla's entire ordnance, experienced in long warfare in the Deccan and served by skilled European gunners. Jaswant, on the other hand, despised fire-arms as unworthy of a heroic race like the Rajputs. Nearly half his army, that is Qasim Khan's Muslim troopers, were in secret league with Aurangzib and turned traitors in the fight. Jaswant also chose his ground very badly; his Rajputs were densely packed in a narrow space with ditches and entrenchments on their flanks, so that they could neither manoeuvre freely nor gather momentum for a charge. His plan was to skirt the enemy's artillery and by a wild gallop came to close quarters with Aurangzib's troops, disregarding the gunfire during the first few minutes of the charge. His post was also within range of the enemy's artillery planted on a higher ground.

Battle Formation

Aurangzib's vanguard was composed of 8000 steel-clad warriors under his eldest son Muhammad Sultan and two very experienced generals, with some divisional guns, The main artillery was ranged before the vanguard. The right wing was formed by Prince Murad Bakhsh's contingent and the left by Multafat Khan (Aurangzib's own men). The centre was led by Aurangzib himself, with Shaikh Mir (right) and Saf Shikan Khan (left) guarding its two flanks with separate corps, this left flank having some guns of its own. The very useful advanced reserve (*iltmish*) consisted of Aurangzib's personal guards, very dependable men. In front of the van spread the skirmishers (*qarawwal*), a loose body of horsemen from the scouts and the men of the royal hunt.

Jaswant's vanguard was in two heavy columns (side by side), totalling 10,000 horsemen. Of these the division of Qasim Khan (4,000) may be written off as non-existent; the other column, composed of Rajputs under Mukund Singh Hada and six other Hindu leaders, did most of the fighting and sacrificed themselves. The centre was led by Jaswant at the head of 2,000 brave Rathors, with other Rajputs in support. His right wing under Rai Singh Sisodia was a Rajput force, and his left under Iftikhar Khan contained Muslim troopers of the imperial service. The advanced reserve was also composed of Rajputs, but the front skirmishers were a body of horse-archers of Central Asia. His artillery was negligible and had no real effect on the fighting.

Battle of Dharmat, 15th April, 1658

Aurangzib, marching slowly and in perfect order, came in sight of the stationary imperial army two hours after sunrise, and at once began to shoot down the Rajputs densely packed in columns, without space to open out. The Rajput losses began to mount every minute. Then their vanguard, led by Mukund Singh Hada, Ratan Singh Rathor and other clan-chieftains, made a wild charge upon Aurangzib's artillery. Sacrificing many men to the point-blank discharge, the remnant pressed on and bore down all opposition, the Prince's chief of artillery was slain and the gunners put to flight. Then the victorious Rajputs fell upon the front ranks of Aurangzib's vanguard. Here an obstinate hand to hand combat raged for some time, and the Rajputs swept onwards and penetrated to the heart of this enemy division.

But Aurangzib's war-hardened troops kept their ground firmly, the chiefs on their elephants, while the Rajput assailants whirled round them like small eddies. In the end the force of Rajput impact was broken on striking the dense mass of Aurangzib's steel-clad troopers and "the ground was dyed crimson with blood."

During the agony of this contest, no reinforcement came to the Rajputs from the main bodies of Jaswant or Qasim Khan, while Aurangzib pushed up his advanced reserve to aid his van and himself came nearer with the centre to back them. The men of his van, at first shaken and pushed back by the wild Rajput charge, now rallied and turning back formed a wall closing the path of retreat to the Rajput attack. The two flanks of Aurangzib's centre advanced ahead of their master and struck this Rajput body in the waist from two sides. Hopelessly outnumbered, assailed in front, right and left, and cut off from the rear, the Rajputs of Mukund Singh and Ratan Singh were slaughtered after performing frantic deeds of valour; all the six chiefs engaged in this charge were slain.

Meantime, Aurangzib's gunners, returning to their pieces after the Rajput flood had swept on to another point of the field, concentrated their fire on Jaswant's centre, where the men "sacrificed their lives like moths in a flame", unable to defend themselves.

When the fortune of war had taken this turn, three captains from the right flank of Jaswant's centre and his vanguard, left the field with their followers and took the way home. Murad Bakhsh had already attacked and taken possession of Jaswant's camp in his rear, and next advancing fell on the left wing of the imperial army, whose commander was slain and his men put to rout.

Jaswant had by this time seen his right, left and van melt away, and his ally Qasim Khan was openly getting ready to leave the field and seek his own safety by submission to Aurangzib. The victorious princes made a convergent move in the three divisions, upon Jaswant's centre. In this hopeless situation Jaswant took to flight, and the battle ended in the utter rout and loss of camp and baggage of the Emperor's army. On the side of the defeated nearly six thousand men fell in the field, being mostly Rajputs; nearly all of their captains were killed and only one Muslim general.

Aurangzib showed the same quickness of movement and spirit of enterprise after this victory as before it. The very day after the battle, he marched 14 miles to Ujjain (16th April), and thence reached Gwalior on 21st May. Here he learnt that his direct road to Agra was barred by Dara Shukoh who had planted guns and run trenches on the bank of the Chambal near Dholpur to deny him a crossing. Aurangzib, therefore, under the guidance of a local zamindar decided to make a detour to Bhadaoli, 40 miles east of Dholpur and there cross the Chambal at an obscure and unguarded ford. The very evening of his arrival at Gwalior, he sent a strong detachment with artillery which by a forced march all night reached this ford next day, crossed over and secured the other bank. The main army under the two princes followed this route in two days, undergoing a loss of 5,000 men (mostly followers) from the hardships of the broken waterless tract. But the strategic success was complete: by this one stroke Dara's elaborate entrenchments and batteries at Dholpur were rendered useless; his enemies were now within easy reach of Agra and he was forced to abandon his heavy guns and fall back on the capital to defend it.

Samugarh, 29th May, 1658

With a newly raised and very raw army Dara gave battle to his brothers on the sandy plain of Samugarh, near the south bank of the Jamuna, 8 miles due east of Agra Fort. His army numbered about 50,000 men. Its backbone was formed by the Rajput contingent and Dara's old retainers, but nearly half of this vast host belonged to the Emperor's service, and these Muslims were jealous of Dara's favour to the Rajputs and secretly in league with Aurangzib, the champion of Islam. Dara's artillery was drawn up in one row along his entire front, behind it stood the foot-musketeers, next the elephants, and last of all the dense masses of cavalry. In opposition to this host stood Aurangzib's veterans and excellent train of field pieces, the men flushed with victory and the officers trained to obey one commander of iron will.

The battle began at a very hot summer noon. After the usual exchange of cannonade, Dara ordered a charge. His left wing under Rustam Khan, issuing in front of his guns, formed a dense column and attacked the opposing artillery. But Aurangzib's ordnance chief Saf Shikan Khan and the musketeers posted behind the guns, stood their ground well and received the charge with one deadly volley, which checked Dara's cavalry and forced Rustam Khan to swerve to his right and try to pierce Aurangzib's vanguard. But Bahadur Khan with the right flank of that prince's centre had hurried up to fill the gap between his artillery and vanguard, and he brought Rustam Khan to a halt. In the close fight that followed, Bahadur Khan fell down wounded, and his division was shaken, but for a moment only; because very soon Islam Khan came to its aid from the right wing and Shaikh Mir with the advanced reserve. In the end Rustam Khan was outnumbered and borne down; he fell dead among a heap of the slain and the small remnant of his band fled back.

At the same time a more terrible and more successful fight was waged against Aurangzib's left. There the Rajputs of the imperial vanguard under Chhatra Sal Hada and Ram Singh Rathor attacked Murad Bakhsh, driving a wedge between the two allied brothers. Murad himself received three wounds and his elephant's *hauda* was stuck full of arrows like a porcupine's back. Ram Singh and many other Rajputs fell in this hand to hand fighting, but Murad's division was borne backwards.

The victorious Rajputs then galloped on the centre and fell upon Aurangzib as he was hastening to the support of Murad. His bodyguard offered a most stubborn defence and the Rajputs, now worn out by toil, sadly thinned in numbers, and mounted on tired horses, were overcome by these fresh men. One by one all the Rajput leaders fell, but their followers made a frantic struggle like "ravening dogs", till all of them perished on the spot.

When the battle opened and Dara's left wing and vanguard rushed to the attack, that prince quitted his position in the centre, rode through his own artillery and went towards Aurangzib's right wing in order to support the charge of Rustam Khan. He thus lost control over his far-flung divisions, there was none left at the centre to give directions and everything fell into confusion. Moreover, in his present position he obstructed the fire of his own artillery, while Aurangzib's guns continued to mow down his men without any chance of reply. The baffled prince turned to his own right in order to avoid the enemy artillery in front of him and reached Shaikh Mir's division (Aurangzib's Advanced Reserve). But he made a short halt before charging, owing to the broken sandy ground and the fatigue of his over-exerted men; thus, his force lost its momentum and the vigour of the intended onslaught was greatly slackened. Seeing the enemy ranks before him fully dressed and ready to repel him, he abandoned his forward movement and turned aside towards his own right wing in order to back Chhatra Sal.

Thus, Dara only made a long movement across his entire front from the extreme left to near the extreme right. The frightful heat and thirst struck down his men and horses during this unprofitable manoeuvre and the survivors were too exhausted to fight.

Then came the last stage of the battle. Aurangzib's vanguard had kept its proper position all this time and husbanded its strength. And now, on seeing Dara's two wings and vanguard overthrown and his centre in disorder and out of its proper place, Aurangzib's vanguard sprang forward to attack Dara, while his right wing wheeled round to envelop that luckless prince, and his batteries from right and left converged their fire on this doomed division. This was the beginning of the end. Dara's own elephant now became a target for the enemy's balls; and so he changed to a horse. At once all was over with him; his troops on seeing his *hauda* empty, concluded that their master had fallen, and they broke and fled away in the utmost disorder.

No victory could be more complete. Ten thousand men had fallen on Dara's side and all his baggage and guns were captured. The havoc among the faithful Rajputs was terrible, 'in the two battles of Dharmat and Samugarh twelve princes of the Hada royal family together with the head of every Hada sub-clan gave up their lives.' The treachery of Khalil-ullah Khan (in command of Dara's right wing) who went over to the enemy during the crisis of the battle, confirmed a victory which was due to superior generalship and better troops.

Battle of Khajwa, 5th Jan., 1659

From Samugarh Dara fled to Agra and thence to the Panjab and Sindh. Aurangzib after his victory took possession of Agra fort, imprisoned his old father, crowned himself Emperor at Delhi (21st July, 1658) and set out for the Panjab on the heels of Dara Shukoh. His other brother Shuja (governor of Bengal and Bihar) had been surprised and routed near Benares (14th February, 1658) by Dara's eldest son. But now, on hearing of Aurangzib's absence with his main troops in the far-off Panjab, Shuja planned an attack upon the undefended Delhi province. So, at the head of 25,000 cavalry and some artillery he started from Patna at the end of October, but moved so slowly as to reach Khajwa in the Fatehpur district, 95 miles north-west of Allahabad on 30th December. Here he found his path barred by Aurangzib's eldest son Sultan Muhammad. In the meantime Aurangzib, on hearing of Shuja's invasion, had hastened back from the Panjab and strongly reinforced his advanced division near Allahabad. On 2nd January, 1659, the Emperor himself joined his son at Kora, eight miles west of Shuja's position, and on the same day Mir Jumla from the Deccan arrived to aid him as his most "faithful friend" (*yar-i-wafadar*). On 4th January, Aurangzib, marching his army in perfect order, arrived one mile in front of Shuja's camp, and the battle was fixed for the morrow.

A few hours before sunrise on that eventful day, Jaswant Singh (Maharaja of Jodhpur), the commander of the imperial right wing, with his 14,000 Rajputs, rose in tumult, deserted his master, and went away looting the part of the imperial camp which lay in his path. Instead of joining Shuja, he took the opposite road to Rajputana. The indescribable confusion and alarm in the imperial army in the darkness was checked and order restored by Aurangzib's coolness and iron will, and the battle began, as planned at 8 o'clock in the morning.

Shuja's 23,000 men were opposed to Aurangzib's 50,000 veterans and fine portable field guns. So, with true generalship he gave up the customary plan of fighting in parallel lines to the enemy, opposing division to division, as his line would have been overlapped and swallowed up by the vastly extended line of his enemy. He decided to assume the offensive and make up for the smallness of his numbers by the moral superiority which an offensive gives.

After an hour spent in the showy exchange of fire, the two vanguards advanced and closed together, plying their arrows. Sayyid Alam, leading Shuja's right wing, charged the imperial left wing, driving in front of himself three infuriated (*mast*) elephants each of which brandished a two-maund iron chain with its trunk. None could stand before them; Aurangzib's left wing broke and fled; the panic spread to his centre where the soldiers began to run about in confusion. As the enemy attack pressed towards the centre, the two reserves on the Emperor's wings flung themselves forward and barred Sayyid Alam's path. Shuja's general was repulsed and fled back to his own lines.

But the three elephants continued to advance wildly, scattering the men before them. One of them came up to Aurangzib's elephant. The Emperor stood like a rock and chained the legs of his own elephant to prevent its flight—which would have been interpreted by his army as the Emperor's flight and admission of defeat! A matchlockman shot down the driver of the attacking elephant and a brave imperial *mahut* nimbly leaped on its back and brought the riderless beast under control. The crisis passed, and the Emperor then turned to succour his right wing which had been hard-pressed by a charge of Shuja's vanguard and left wing under Prince Buland Akhtar, and thrown into confusion.

But even in the greatest danger, Aurangzib's presence of mind did not desert him. It at once struck him that as his own front had hitherto been turned towards the left, if he were now to face *suddenly* to the right, the army would interpret this *volte face* as his flight. So he first sent couriers to reassure his brigadiers and then wheeled the centre round in support of his right wing, just in time to save it. This was the decisive move of the day, and thenceforth the tide of battle rolled resistlessly against Shuja. The imperial right made a countercharge and swept away the enemy before it with dreadful slaughter.

Meantime the imperial vanguard under Zulfiqar Khan had beaten back the attack upon it, advanced and shaken the enemy's front. Preceded by a most destructive fire from Aurangzib's side, the entire imperial army made a general advance, and enveloped Shuja's centre, his two wings having been scattered before. Shuja, in imminent danger of being shot down, got down from his elephant and took horse. His army broke and took to flight, believing that their master was dead. Everything fell to the victors.

Chapter XVII

WAR FOR THE DELHI THRONE: JAJAU, 1707

The battle of Jajau, which was fought only three months after Aurangzib's death, between two of his sons, differed entirely in its character from the three great battles by which that Emperor had won his father's throne, fifty years earlier, (as described in Chapter XVI). First, the campaign was marked by the utter want of generalship; it was a soldiers' battle, or rather a sectional commanders' affairs, with no planning or concerted action by a supreme leader. Secondly, here the issue was entirely dominated by guns and muskets, and the old Turkish tactics hitherto followd in Hindustan, had no room for play. Jajau revealed a degeneracy in the Mughal imperial army, as regards organisation and conduct of war, which truly foreboded the disaster of Nadir Shah's victory thirty years later.

When Aurangzib died (20th Feb., 1707) his eldest surviving son Muazzam, surnamed Shah Alam (and crowned as Bahadur Shah I) was the governor of Kabul. On hearing of his father's death he made a rapid march from Jamrud (in the Khyber Pass) to Agra (arriving outside that city on 2nd June). His strength consisted in his four sons, all grown up and experienced in affairs and except one all very able and spirited,—a large band of competent and devoted officers, all the accumulated treasure of the house of Babur, hoarded in Agra fort, and an overpowering force of artillery, served partly by European and mestizo gunners.

Against him came up from the Deccan his younger brother Muhammad Azam Shah, a brave but insanely proud and hot-headed old man (aged 62), who disgusted his best followers and weakened himself by his senseless jealousy of his own son Bidar Bakht,—the ablest and most war-hardened grandson of Aurangzib. Azam's army was numerically less than half that of Bahadur Shah, and by an act of utter folly and ignorance of the march of time, he left all his guns behind, and faced his elder brother with a few hand-guns and rockets only, which proved mere playthings. All the slaughter among Azam's family and officers was caused by his enemy's fire-arms.

Prince Azam, after reaching Gwalior on 2nd June, sent his vanguard 25,000 strong ahead, the front part commanded by his eldest son Bidar Bakht and the supports by a younger son Wala-Jah, while he himself followed one day's march behind. After crossing the Chambal at the Kaimthri ferry, six miles due south of Dholpur city, his army pushed northwards towards Agra by the old Mughal King's highway (*Shah-rah*) from the Deccan. The present railway line from Dholpur runs parallel to this road.

Agra lies 36 miles due north of Dholpur in a straight line. The old royal road after leaving Akbar's capital comes to its first halting stage at Tehra, 14 miles south-west; a little beyond the crossing of the Khari Nadi. Six miles further south the river Utangan has to be crossed at the village of Jajau. Here a *sarai* stood on the river bank for travellers to wait when the wide sandy bed of the snaky river was suddenly flooded by heavy rain. A bridge was built here, but later than our battle, and today there is a small station named Jajau where the railway line crosses the river, but it is a mile east of the old village of the name. Proceeding eight miles to the south we come to Mania, the largest place between Agra and Dholpur, and eight miles beyond it stands the old city of Dholpur, with the nearest point of the Chambal river two miles further south.

The field of battle can be best traced from the diary of Bhimsen Burhanpuri, who was present at it in Azam's ranks and wrote his book soon afterwards. Bahadur Shah set out from the garden of Daharara (popularly pronounced Dhara) in the western suburbs of Agra, to reach the Chambal, 38 miles south of him. On the same day Prince Azam started from Gwalior, and by a quick march crossed the Chambal near Dholpur and pursued the same route *northwards* to Agra. Each army advanced, in a huge sprawling body or rather a long chain of columns, without sending scouts in advance and quite in the dark about its enemy's position. But a head-on collision between them was averted by the fact that Bahadur Shah from Agra kept to the *west* of the highway (i.e., the modern railway) and inclined towards Khairagarh, while Azam Shah chose the *eastern* side of the same path (inclining towards Iradatnagar), because his objective was not Agra city but Samugarh, six miles due east of the capital. Thus the two armies came to move in parallel lines, with a space of four miles east to west separating them, when they first came in contact.

In the morning of 8th June, Bidar Bakht, with his father's vanguard, resumed his advance from his night's halting place near Jajau. After two hours of painful marching through dust, sand and raging thirst, he reached a village, about four miles north-east of Jajau, halted there, because of its good water supply, and sent word to his father, who was coming up three miles behind. The troops of the vanguard were scattered and its few guns were left miles behind, because no fighting was expected that day. Even the different corps of the vanguard marched carelessly as they pleased without battle dress or order, because of the heat and sandy broken ground; Zulfiqar Khan, in command of Bidar Bakht's left flank, strayed so far away as to be out of sight of his chief.

That morning, from the other side, Bahadur Shah had begun his southward march in equal ignorance of his enemy's position, and sent off his advanced tents under escort of his son Azim-ush-Shan to be erected in a grove four miles north of Jajau, and himself with his three other sons and the main army made a detour to hunt on the way. The troops of Bidar Bakht moving northwards saw these tents with imperial pennons on their left front. Khan-i-Alam Deccani and his brother Munavvar Khan detached themselves from Bidar Bakht's left wing and fell upon the party erecting the tents. Though they were only 2,500 strong, the suddenness of their attack drove away most of Azim-ush-Shan's troops, so that he had only 450 horsemen left out of his 25,000 men to support him. In the confusion the royal tents were set on fire and their guardian the Mir Tuzak was captured.

But while Khan-i-Alam's men dispersed for plunder, Azim-ush-Shan stood firmly facing the enemy and calling up reinforcements from his father on his own right rear. On seeing Bahadur Shah's own elephant running away with its royal *hauda* riderless, Bidar Bakht's scouts reported that the Emperor had been slain, and that prince advanced towards Azim-ush-Shan, beating his drums for the imagined victory. But on reaching the place he found his path barred by nearly one lakh of troopers, against his own 20,000, for two full divisions of the Emperor's army—one under the Wazir Munim Khan and the second under two other Shahzadas, had by this time joined Azim-ush-Shan and placed a line of guns in their front. "On Bidar Bakht's side it was found impossible to rally all his men, many of whom had dispersed to plunder the royal camp. His troops were also hampered by the crowd of baggage elephants, cattle and followers on both flanks and in their rear." He had no artillery. While thus brought to a halt, Bidar Bakht's men were helplessly slaughtered by his opponent's artillery; "the musketry balls fell like hail, and the rockets placed in a line before the advancing troops were repeatedly discharged with effect." (Irvine).

"The sun was high in the heavens and the heat excessive. After a time Bidar Bakht's men became impatient and made ready to charge, headed by Khan-i-Alam Deccani and his body-guard of 500 men." But only three hundred of them remained with him to the end of the charge. Khan-i-Alam on his elephant forced his way to Azim-ush-Shan and attacked him, but he was surrounded by tenfold odds and killed, and his brother Munavvar Khan wounded; then the remnant of his party broke and fled away.

Meantime, Prince Wala-Jah with his own division had pushed on from behind Bidar Bakht to his left front to support his elder brother. After the fall of Khan-i-Alam his isolated position became too dangerous; Amanullah Khan who had hastened to Wala-Jah's support from the main body of Bidar Bakht, fell down half-burnt by a rocket, and the younger prince retreated for protection to the vanguard.

At the same time a corps of Azim-ush-Shan had attacked Zulfiqar Khan who commanded the large left flank of Bidar Bakht. Though Zulfiqar repulsed the attack, two of his ablest and most trusted commanders, Ram Singh Hada of Bundi and Dalpat Rao Bundela were killed by cannon-shot. "The Rajputs lost heart and fled, taking with them the dead bodies of their chieftains." A little later, Zulfiqar on being assailed by the whole force of Azim-ush-Shan's division took to flight. So also did Sawai Jai Singh of Jaipur, a favourite of Bidar Bakht, who hid himself in his *hauda* and thus went over to the enemy opposite. Despair and relaxation seized Bidar Bakht's men. "The heat was excessive, the soil sandy and a hot wind arose which blew the burning sand into his soldiers' faces. The leaders on his side dismounted and awaited the enemy's charge, resolved to sell their lives dearly. On the other (i.e., Emperor's) side the Sayyids of Barha, equally determined to do or die, advanced to the attack on foot." After a desperate fight most of Bidar Bakht's commanders were slain and a large number of Bahadur Shah's supporters killed and wounded; the two Sayyid brothers, who were to be king-makers in the next reign, were so severely wounded as to be left for dead.

At last a ball from a swivel-gun killed Bidar Bakht who had already been wounded by arrows. Prince Wala-Jah who had arrived to reinforce his elder brother, lost many officers in this long and unequal struggle. Fainting from repeated wounds he was at last driven off on his elephant to the rear and taken to his father Azam Shah. It was now only three hours to sunset. The main body under Azam Shah in person, now took up the contest, which raged for two hours more. His chief captains fell thick and fast around him from the enemy's fire to which he could make no reply, and most others were wounded. "Azam Shah in spite of the death of his eldest son and of so many leaders, urged on his elephant, amidst a rain of arrows and balls, into the thick of the fight. One after another four drivers of his elephant were shot down." And then he tried to direct the beast by pushing his leg out of the *hauda* and pressing its head with his toes! "He was struck several times, but paid no heed to his wounds. At length a musket ball struck him on the forehead and killed him.... It was then about one and a half hours before nightfall. His flying troops made off towards Gwalior, and so many lost their lives on the way at the hands of Jat plunderers and the Ruhelas of Dholpur, that the ravines leading to the Chambal were encumbered with decaying bodies." Prince Wala-Jah also expired in the field from his wounds.

The loss on the two sides taken together was roughly estimated at ten thousand men and many hundreds of horses and scores of elephants perished from heat and thirst, exhaustion and wounds. Of the dead on Azam Shah's side in the field, the officers, high and low, were probably as many as one-tenth of the common soldiers. This shows the disadvantage under which this party fought.

Chapter XVIII

NIZAM-UL-MULK'S THREE BATTLES: RATANPUR

Nizam-ul-Mulk Asaf Jah, the founder of the Haidarabad dynasty, came of a very noble Turkish family of Central Asia, and migrated to India with his father and grand-father in Aurangzib's reign. Here all the three rose to the highest posts and honours by their extraordinary talents. The father (entitled Ghaziuddin Firuz Jang) was one of the two highest nobles of that Emperor. Asaf Jah himself (original titles, Mir Qamruddin, Chin Qilich Khan, and Fath Jang) was the best Muslim general in India during the first half of the 18th century; but his statesmanship and administrative capacity were even greater than his military genius. In the power of planning, commanding men, and managing intricate affairs with tact and promptitude, he was far above his rivals. As the English factors of Madras noted in February, 1744, he preferred diplomatic agreement to war, and he always confirmed the fruits of his victories by his moderation and courtesy to the vanquished.

The Emperor Muhammad Shah (who reigned from 1719 to 1748) had been set up on the throne of Delhi by two all-powerful Ministers, the Sayyid Brothers, Husain Ali and Abdullah, in whose hands he was a mere puppet, as he had neither the strength of will nor character. These two Ministers were Indian Muslims (settled in 'Barah' in the Muzaffarnagar district of the United Provinces) and Shias by religion. Nizam-ul-Mulk was a Sunni and the leader of the foreign Turkish soldiery in India.

The Sayyid Brothers filled all the important posts with their own men, and being jealous of the superior ability and power of Nizam, they plotted to crush him, lest he should assert his independence and oust them from the Emperor's regency.

In March, 1719, Nizam was sent to Malwa (capital, Ujjain) as its Subahdar. But the two king-makers plotted to remove and imprison him. So, early next year they sent an order from the Emperor recalling him to Delhi and appointing their own man Sayyid Dilawwar Ali as Subahdar of the province. At the same time another partisan of the Ministers, named Sayyid Alim Ali, the Subahdar of the Deccan, was ordered to march northwards from his seat Aurangabad and attack Nizam.

To avoid being crushed between these two enemies, Nizam-ul-Mulk decided to strike the first blow before they could unite. Leaving Ujjain, he crossed the Narmada on 8th May, 1720, and seized the city of Burhanpur (the capital of Khandesh subah) with its fort of Asirgarh, midway between Malwa and the Deccan.

Alim Ali began his northward march from Aurangabad about 10th June with a large force. At the same time, Dilawwar Ali, moving southwards, crossed the Narmada and reached Husainpur, 14 kos from Burhanpur. Nizam did not lose a minute. Leaving his family and treasure in Asir fort for safety, he marched out of Burhanpur on 15th June to meet Dilawwar Ali first. Near Ratanpur (in the Handiya sub-division of the Hoshangabad district) he contacted the enemy.

Natives' Crass Stupidity

In this contest the core of Nizam's army consisted of Mughalias, that is Turks of Central Asia and Persians, and all his commanders were foreign Muslims. His officers formed a more enlightened and cleverer body of military leaders than the chiefs of the opposite side who were brave, no doubt, but no better than rustics. These foreign group-commanders had the intelligence and education to put their followers' courage to the best use and co-ordinate the work of the different brigades so as to derive the utmost benefit from the men's exertions. Dilawwar Ali's army was purely Indian in its composition,—Rajputs, Ruhelas and the Sayyid clansmen of the Muzaffarnagar district.

The Rajputs are characterized in the Persian histories of Delhi by 'jahalat-i-markaz' or crass stupidity. The Indo-Afghans were no better; Babur in his 'Memoirs' illustrates their rustic ignorance. As for the Sayyids of Barha, in North Indian popular speech the term was a byword for blunt ignorance and pride. Thus Dilawwar Ali's men fought only with blind fury and animal courage, and not with their brains; each section of his men advanced individually against the foe immediately in front of itself and gave no thought to the plans and situation of its comrades in other parts of the field.

Nizam's superiority in numbers was greatly enhanced by the excellence of his artillery, the ability of his officers, and the efficiency of his organisation. His artillery had been taken over from his father Firuz Jang's, whose number, fulness of equipment and 'material,' and efficiency and discipline had excited the jealousy and alarm of Aurangzib twenty years earlier. That suspicious Emperor had warned his grandson (in 1702), "The muster of armament which Khan Firuz Jang showed to me contained guns, elephant-swivels, camel-swivels, horse-swivels, and all other kinds of firearms, not only as many as he is bound to maintain according to his pay and rank, but far more than that. Why do you, who are getting double his salary, waste your money, with nothing to show in return for it?" (Maasir-i-Alamgiri, 278).

Battle Of Ratanpur

Hearing of Nizam's close approach, Dilawwar Ali made his arrangements for fighting him. He occupied a plateau west of the northward highway, and depositing his camp and baggage for safety in a low ground two miles behind it, made trenches and posted artillery so as to mow down his enemy's troops as they advanced to the attack. Nizam encamped four miles south of this position, and the next day, 9th June, 1720, was fixed for the battle.

In the morning of that day, as the Sayyid General waited in his chosen field in proud confidence of victory, his spies brought the report that the enemy had broken camp and was marching away elsewhere. This move he interpreted as a panic flight of Nizam and the boastful talk and merriment in the Sayyid's camp became still more boisterous. But about noonday his spies gave him a news as incredible "as if the Sun had risen in the west instead of in the east" (—for so the Persian history aptly puts it); it was that Nizam's standards were seen four miles in the 'west,' approaching the rear of the Sayyid's position. In fact, Nizam had, by one stroke of military genius, nullified all the plans of his enemy. Wisely judging a frontal attack from a lower ground on such a well-prepared position to be suicidal, he made a detour to reach the enemy's unguarded rear. Leaving the familiar highway north of him, he struck into the trackless fields on his left and after marching 12 miles appeared at the back of Dilawwar Ali, a little after midday.

The Sayyid was forced to leave his carefully-prepared trenches and heavy artillery behind, face round from the east to the west, and hasten to his own rear to meet the threat. Only a few light pieces, or swivels borne on elephants and camels could accompany him, and he was forced to fight on the ground of his enemy's choosing and leave the tactical initiative to him.

It was late in the afternoon of 9th June, 1720, when the two armies came into contact. A tract of rugged difficult ground lay between them, scored by many dry 'nalas' over which the path ran between broken jungly banks. Thus at first neither side could deploy its full strength and fight a regular battle in two parallel lines, each division of the one facing the corresponding division of the other force. Only the two vanguards could engage. Dilawwar Ali's men, in addition to having no artillery of their own, were further handicapped by having to advance into unreconnoitred ground. Nizam's officers with great intelligence and promptitude utilised their earlier arrival on the scene by planting their guns in such a way as to sweep the only path of their enemy's advance and posting groups of musketeers in the bushes on both sides of it. They thus formed a death-trap into which the Sayyid's men blindly rushed.

The battle began with a clash between the front lines after a short firing. Sayyid Sher Khan and Sayyid Babar Khan commanding Dilawwar's vanguard, delivered the attack with 2,000 horsemen and 7,000 infantry, supported by 2,000 Rajputs and 3,000 Ruhelas on their right hand. Iwaz Khan, commanding Nizam-ul-Mulk's right wing and Ghiyas Khan his vanguard, advanced to oppose them. But the broken ground prevented these two corps from uniting, and at first the full force of the attack fell on Iwaz Khan, whose front was not protected by artillery. The impetuous charge of the two Sayyids seemed to carry everything before them. Iwaz Khan's elephant was daunted by the fire-flash and wild cries of the mob before it and turned tail, and most of his followers took to flight.

The Khan, however, turned his face to the back of his mount and did all he could to rally his men, exhorting them and shooting arrows though himself wounded. His Turki horsemen stopped in their flight, gathered in small knots and renewed the battle. Reinforcements were pushed up to them from the great reserve in their centre (under Nizam-ul-Mulk himself) and wings. The two Sayyid captains, who had been pursuing Iwaz with shouts of exultation, were checked. The tide of battle ebbed and flowed as each side received fresh troops and made a new dash. At last the two Sayyid leaders were killed and their division ceased to exist.

At the same time from Dilawwar Ali's right wing, two thousand Rajputs (under Budh Singh of Bundi and Gaj Singh of Marwar) and some three thousand Afghans under Ali Muhammad Ruhela, had fallen on Ghiyas Khan who commanded Nizam-ul-Mulk's vanguard and artillery. Here sword and spear failed before cannon and musketry, and in the end, the Rajputs took to their last desperate tactics, got down from their horses and fought on foot till they were killed. Their dead formed heaps in that contracted space; four hundred corpses were counted out of their contingent of 2,000. The Ruhelas saved themselves by flight.

As soon as the fighting became general, Dilawwar Ali at the head of his main body, at least 6,000 strong, started from the centre and drove his elephant impetuously towards Nizam-ul-Mulk, who was standing with his escort, reduced to 600 men by the heavy reinforcement that he had detached to the front line. As he came up, a bullet grazed the Sayyid's forehead and threw him into a swoon; his chin sank down on his knees, and his driver led the elephant back to an open space in the rear. Here Dilawwar Ali revived and once more drove his elephant on to encounter Nizam, who had halted beside a 'nala.'

This time another bullet pierced his abdomen and finished his career. Most of his captains had already fallen, and the battle ended in two hours with the total ruin of his army.

The loss on Dilawwar Ali's side was estimated as four thousand men and all the leaders killed and at least twice that number wounded. In Nizam-ul-Mulk's army 30 men (of whom only two were officers) fell and a hundred were wounded.

Greatest Indian General

All the three battles of Nizam-ul-Mulk have some features in common which mark him out as the greatest Indian general of the 18th century. He defeated superior numbers of enemies, his victories were decisive and annihilated the opposing army, and his successes were gained by a remarkable economy of men, the enemy's losses being sometimes ten times his own. This result was due mainly to his own towering genius for organisation, choice of instruments, and quick decision in field tactics. But he also owed much to his more efficient and modernised artillery and the galaxy of able and educated lieutenants gathered round him, each of whom was capable of independent command and of seizing the initiative without waiting for orders. No other Indian army had so many corps-commanders of such rare capacity. His transport system was more efficient and faster than that of the rustic Sayyids.

He had inferior numbers in each of his battles, but the enemy attacked and he waited for them, in a prepared position, the advantage of which was doubled by his power to use his big guns, while the moving enemy outstripped their own guns. When the two sides are equal in armament and civilisation, the attack must be thrice as strong in number, if it is to bear down the defence.

Nizam-ul-Mulk's forces were better trained, held under admirable control, and their action co-ordinated by a master mind from the safe rear (really centre), while the troops attacking him had to be led by their highest officers, with whose fall they broke and fled.

The sun went down as the fighting ended. Nizam-ul-Mulk did not allow a pursuit, but husbanded his forces and attended to the wounded. Next morning a force of 3,000 chosen cavalry from his camp made a memorable dash of 80 miles in 24 hours and reached Burhanpur, where the families and property of his soldiers had been left behind without defenders. They were thus saved from Alim Ali who was advancing on that town from the south.

Chapter XIX

NIZAM-UL-MULK'S THREE BATTLES: BALAPUR AND SHAKAR KHERA

Sayyid Alim Ali, the nephew and agent of the Sayyid Brothers in the Deccan, was a youth of 22, brave to rashness but possessing neither generalship nor capacity for management. He failed in his first task of joining Dilawwar Ali in time to crush Nizam-ul-Mulk by a concerted attack. In contrast with Nizam's prompt decision and rapid movements, both these Sayyid generals were hopelessly slow. It was 9th May, 1720, before Alim Ali started from Aurangabad. While he was only halfway to Burhanpur (Nizam-ul-Mulk's base) his enemy had already crushed Dilawwar Ali (9th June) and reinforced Burhanpur. Thereafter the Sayyid general moved about aimlessly in bewilderment, and only tried to raise more followers and seduce Nizam's partisans. He made a long halt south of the Purna river (Hartala Lake, 5 m. s. w. of Adilabad), his men suffering much hardship from the rain and flooded rivers. Nizam lay encamped on the north bank of the same river, enduring similar hardships from the weather. At last he made a sudden strategic move eastwards up the river and crossed the Purna unhindered at an easy ford away from his enemy. The two armies were now on the same bank and Alim Ali moved eastwards to meet him. After a further spell of inactivity due to the foul weather, Nizam-ul-Mulk reached Balapur in Berar (by way of Shegaon) and forced a battle at a place, five miles from Balapur city on 31st July, 1720.

Nizam's Army

Nizam's army was mainly composed of foreign Muslims—Iranis and Turanis, popularly called Mughals,—while Alim Ali had come from the south at the head of 30,000 men, one half of whom were Karnataki horsemen and the other made up of various groups of Indo-Muslim troops, such as his own Sayyid clansmen and many bands of Afghan mercenaries, settled in the Deccan; and he was also accompanied by a vast horde of Maratha light horse, popularly estimated at 17,000 men, whom Raja Shahu of Satara had sent under his Senapati Khandoji Dhabare to support the Government of Delhi. These allies had no influence on the fighting, they merely followed the Maratha game of looting the enemy's baggage while the soldiers were busy in combat.

The vanguard of Nizam-ul-Mulk was commanded by Muhammad Ghiyas and strengthened by his artillery under Muhammad Shah. His right wing was under the tried and trusty Iwaz Khan, centre under his son Ghaziuddin, and rear under Rao Rambha Nimbalkar, a Maratha chief hostile to the house of Shahu.

Alim Ali's vanguard, consisted of 15,000 Karnataki horse-musketeers under Tahawwar Khan Afghan, seventeen war-elephants, and his park of artillery under Ghiyasuddin. He himself occupied the centre, while his Maratha allies hovered on his left wing.

Nizam-ul-Mulk was the first to advance to the attack. The Sayyid's artillery was ineffective, but the first shot fired by Nizam knocked down the *hauda* of Latif Khan's elephant. Before the smoke could clear, Tahawwar Khan with his elephants and a vast horde of Karnataki horsemen fell impetuously on Nizam's vanguard and threw it into great disorder, many of the men being forced into flight. After an obstinate fight in which many of their officers were wounded, this division retreated.

But in the meantime other divisions from the right and left of Nizam-ul-Mulk's army had advanced to the attack and hemmed the assailants round. Alim Ali, on his part, pushed forward the centre of his army in such hurry that a portion of it was left behind. Nizam-ul-Mulk's tried generals repelled Alim Ali, wherever he turned. Other brave captains of the Mughalias sustained the fight against the Sayyid's elephants though wounded. In this confused and mixed combat, Alim Ali was wounded; a little later his elephant-driver was killed; other leaders also fell,—Ghiyasuddin Khan (his chief of artillery), Tahawwar Khan Afghan (the commander of his van-guard) and seven other high officers.

Left unsupported in an advanced position, Alim Ali's elephant being unable to bear the rain of arrows any longer, at first turned tail. But three times did the youthful Sayyid general return to the combat, his wounds dripping blood. In the end, however, nothing could prevent a retreat before his swarm of well-led and well-combined enemies. While still fighting a hopeless rearguard fight he was again and again wounded and at last surrounded and killed. Seventeen noted chiefs, "riders on elephants," fell on his side and a large number of common soldiers. Many more were wounded. Six hundred and thirty-four Marathas were slain.

On the side of Nizam only four minor officers were killed and six officers wounded. The sword and shield of the Indian Muslims were no match for the Central Asian bow in the hands of expert horsemen, mounted on spirited steeds; our elephants again proved a vain hope, and a more modernised artillery silenced our old guns and gunners.

Shakar Khera, 1724

The battle of Balapur (31 July, 1720) was followed by more changes in the ever-changing Court of the Emperor. The two Sayyid dictators fell, in September and November of that year, and Nizam-ul-Mulk was appointed Prime Minister (Feb. 10, 1722). But the young Emperor was without character or intelligence; he listened easily to Nizam's rivals who wished to crush him by whispering that he was planning to depose the Emperor and crown a boy-prince as his puppet. The Rajput and Hindustani-Muslim nobles were leagued against Nizam-ul-Mulk as the head of the Mughalia or foreign party. These intrigues led to Nizam abandoning the *Wazir*-ship in disgust and retiring to the Deccan, where he reached Aurangabad, the seat of his viceroyalty in July, 1724. His enemies at Court issued an order, signed by the Emperor, appointing Mubariz Khan (then Governor of Golkonda subah) as Viceroy of all Mughal Deccan, displacing Nizam-ul-Mulk, and granted him five lakhs for raising an army. In July Nizam was formally dismissed from the *Wazir*-ship.

Mubariz Khan was a veteran general of the Turkish race, now over sixty years of age. He was at first for prudently waiting on developments, but his hands were forced by his Pathan allies, the Afghan mercenary bands, settled in many places of the Deccan who had formerly been the backbone of the army of the Bijapur Sultans. Therefore, he set out on invasion at the very height of the rainy season. Marching northwestwards from his seat of Haidarabad and crossing the Godavari near Nander, he reached the Char Thana district by way of Basim (in Berar Balaghat) and encamped on the bank of the Purna, somewhere south of the Lonar Lake.

Nizam-ul-Mulk met the challenge by rapidly marching up with a very select force of 6,000 horse and a powerful artillery eastwards from Aurangabad (*C* 23 Aug.) via Jaina, to a place some 22 miles west of Mubariz Khan's encampment. The Khan had a superiority of three to one in numbers, but no artillery. So, instead of attacking Nizam there, he planned a swift strategic blow at the enemy's headquarters far in the rear. He would make a surprise night march, skirting Nizam's camp on the south and west and reach the friendly town of Jafarabad, undetected, and then with fresh allies gathered there he would suddenly fall upon Nizam's unguarded base at Aurangabad, some 65 miles south-west of it, while Nizam's army would be held up near Lonar.

The plan was foiled by the natural slackness and inefficiency of the Indo-Muslim army and the sleepless activity of Nizam's Maratha allies. Mubariz Khan's movement was detected and opposed as soon as it started, and after eight days of skirmishing he was forced to retreat and concentrate his army under the shelter of the fortified town of Shakar Khera. On his part, Nizam-ul-Mulk, by a grim determination and able management, crossed the Purna river to its east bank with all his artillery and stores and followed his enemy up to Shakar Khera.

A look at the map will illustrate these movements. 'Shakar Khera' (renamed 'Fath Khera' by Nizam-ul-Mulk after his victory) is 16 miles n.n.w. of Lonar Lake and 12 miles west of Mehkar on the Pain Ganga. The Purna river flows 20 miles south and also west of Shakar Khera. 'Char Thana' stands 25 m. south of Lonar. 'Jafarabad' is 25 miles due west of Shakar Khera, and 65 m. north-east of Aurangabad. In Irvine's 'Later Mughals,' II. 143, this place is named "Zafarnagar", evidently by mistake.

The Core Of Nizam's Army

The core of Nizam's army was formed by six thousand choice cavalry, mostly Turks and Persians, mounted on good horses, with a large park of artillery, including camel-swivels and easily portable light pieces besides large field guns. These were distributed among his two main divisions, instead of being massed in one place before the vanguard. Thus his divisional commanders could shift and work their artillery quickly and with deadly effect to convenient points with every change in the tide of battle. Mubariz Khan had some light swivel guns or falconets and only two or three large pieces, which were too old and cumbrous and had no effect on the enemy.

But Nizam-ul-Mulk's chief strength lay in his body of highly intelligent war-seasoned brigadiers and captains each of whom knew how to seize the initiative as soon as the need arose with the fighting in any sector taking a new turn. A Greek ambassador described the ancient Senate of Rome as a council of kings. We may similarly call Nizam's entire force as a corps of captains. In contrast with it, Mubariz Khan's army was a body of hot-headed rustics, brave to rashness but ill-armed, ill-led, and never combined at all. It was as if village quarter-staff champions were sacrificing themselves by rushing upon linked battalions firing grape shot.

Battle Formation

Nizam's battle formation followed the European plan rather than the conventional Mughal Indian order. First, he made two main divisions of his men, one under himself and the other on his left hand under Iwaz Khan, each with its own artillery. Secondly, instead of massing his men in two dense bodies in the centre and the reserve, he split them up into many small bands each under an able captain who could be relied upon to combine with others at the right moment

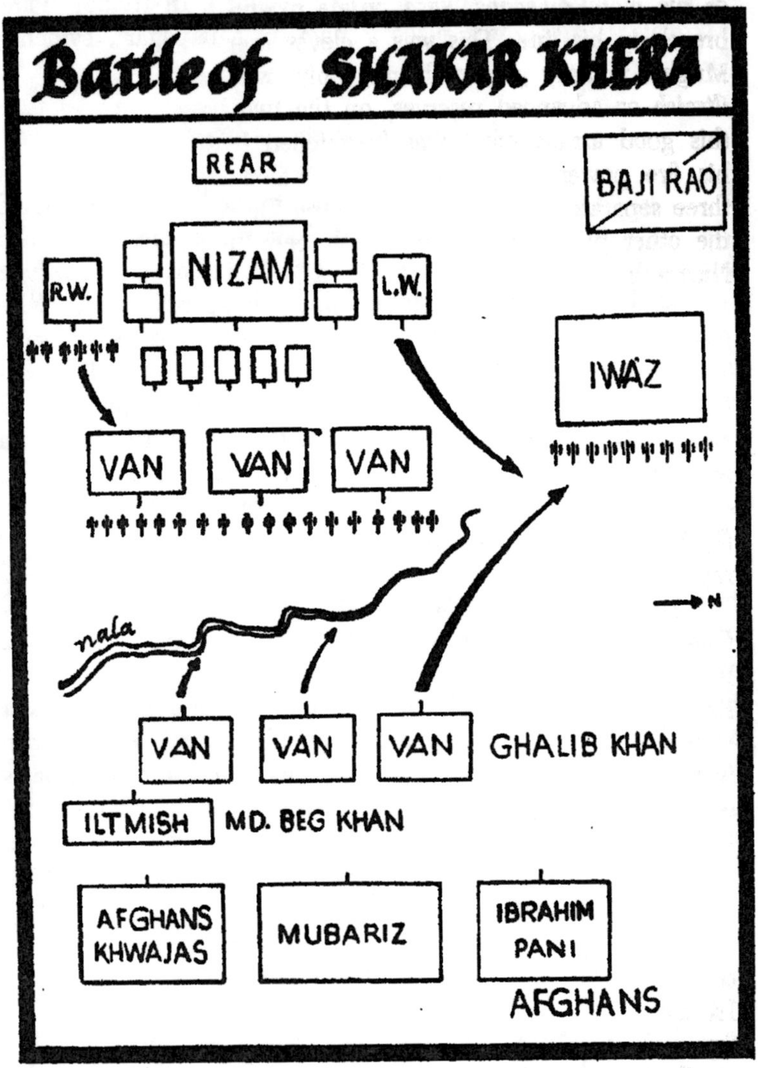

and help in enveloping the enemy's attacking column. Thus there was not the risk of one single wing of his army being shattered and driven out of the field by a desperate push of the enemy's full force. While Nizam-ul-Mulk himself occupied the heart of the centre, some fifteen small bands of horsemen were posted like islands on his front and two flanks, as supports of his main divisions, with orders to rush and patch up any breach in his line. This was a clever improvement on the old Mughal military plan of having only two large reserves, called *iltmish* or advanced reserves, on the two wings. The effect of this good arrangement was heightened by Nizam distributing his fire power (guns and muskets) along his entire front in three separate divisions like the letter U, one with the van and the other two with his ring wing and Iwaz Khan's force (on Nizam-ul-Mulk's Left).

Nizam-ul-Mulk's vanguard was led by Qadir Dad Khan (with the heavy artillery and musketeers), his right wing by Talib Muhiuddin Khan (with light guns and wall-pieces), his left wing by Ismail Khan. He himself occupied the centre, surrounded by many smaller bands in the form of dispersed reserve (*iltmish*). On the left was drawn up Iwaz Khan's division, with its own artillery, while the Maratha light horse (7,000 under Baji Rao, accompanied by Turk-taz Khan, Nizam's representative) stood in the left rear.

Mubariz Khan gave the command of his vanguard to Ghalib Khan, of his advanced reserve (*iltmish* in one body just behind the vanguard) to Muhammad Beg Khan, right wing to Ibrahim Khan Pani (with his 2,000 Indo-Afghan cavalry), left wing to his own sons and the Miana Pathans of the Deccan (more as a part of the centre than as a detached wing); the centre was under himself.

Fighting Develops

Nizam-ul-Mulk waited in his position with his guns chained together and reserving their fire. A little after mid-day, on 1st October, 1724, Mubariz Khan advanced to the attack. He first sent about 9,000 horsemen to fall upon Iwaz Khan. The assailants quickened their pace till they suddenly reached a water-course (*nala*), full of sticky black mud, which lay between. Men and horses began to sink in it and the pressure of the rear ranks threw this force into one dense mass in helpless disorder. Iwaz Khan's artillery worked havoc among them, but the left section of the attacking column, on finding a dry path fell "like roaring tigers" on the right wing and advanced centre of Iwaz Khan and began a hand to hand combat. Many of them had lost their horses or left them behind in the *nala*.

While the assault was thus halted, Nizam's other generals arrived to the rescue of Iwaz and did great execution with their swivel-guns and muskets. Ghalib Khan (the commander of Mubariz's vanguard) was slain, and after standing this pitiless fire of shot and bullet without the means of replying, for an hour and a half, Mubariz's sons Asad and Masaud were killed. On hearing of it their brave father, set his face on a soldier's death and drove his elephant along with the Pathan allies of his right wing into the thick of the fighting. He fought on for nearly another hour; "he had been wounded and his strength began to fail; at times he fainted, but reviving he seized again the bow and arrow. His elephant-driver was killed, he took the dead-man's place and fought on as before. But an hour before sunset Mubariz Khan and all his chief men had lost their lives."

The total losses on Mubariz Khan's side are said to have amounted to 3,500 men, of whom some 30 to 40 were leaders and "riders on elephants." Two of his own sons were slain and two more were wounded and taken prisoners. On Nizam-ul-Mulk's side only three captains fell and his losses in common soldiers did not exceed a few hundreds.

Mubariz Khan had reached Shakar Khera six days before Nizam and yet he had not cared to reconnoitre the ground over which his enemy was advancing even within a mile of his own camp, before setting out to give battle! This scene of helpless massacre of horsemen involved in the sticky black cotton soil of Berar by artillery posted on the other side of an undetected *nala* has a historic parallel in the defeat of Malik Ambar by Shah Nawaz Khan (son of Jahangir's Khan-i-Khanan) on the Godavari, 6th Feb., 1614. (See my *House of Shivaji*, p. 17).

Chapter XX

BAJI RAO'S PALKHED CAMPAIGN

The three victories of Nizam-ul-Mulk over the Delhi forces, already described, prove his genius as the foremost general of his times in India and the efficacy of his war-machine against other Indo-Muslim armies. In these battles the two sides followed the same method of war and differed only in the quality of their leadership. But Nizam-ul-Mulk failed altogether and had to admit defeat when he was opposed by an altogether different system of war, namely, the light foray tactics of the Marathas under Baji Rao I, the ablest exponent of that system. The Palkhed campaign of 1727-28 is worth studying, because it clearly illustrates the difference between the two systems in their result.

This campaign will also repay study by students of Indian Military History, because unlike all other campaigns before the British regime, every day's marching stage of Baji Rao is known to us with its date from the Maratha official diaries. We can thus accurately calculate the miles daily covered by the Maratha horsemen, the impediments on the way that they overcame, and the length of time they could march without rest, and contrast them in these respects with the regular army of the Mughals as led by Nizam. It should not be forgotten that Baji Rao moved without any artillery, baggage or even hand-guns, his troops being armed only with the sword and the long lance (a few with bows also). His men were a purely mounted force, with one led horse to every two troopers; they did not encumber themselves with bulky articles of booty, but merely looted cash and ornaments and burnt the houses along their track. Nizam-ul-Mulk's army was strong in heavy cavalry (many mail-clad); they carried with themselves guns, tents and camp-followers,—so that they always painfully lagged behind the fleet Marathas.

As regards the strategy of this campaign, each side tried to threaten its enemy's capital and thus compel the latter to desist from pillage and return to its own homeland. In this game Nizam took Poona and Baji Rao did not seize Aurangabad; but in the end Baji Rao was more successful and he could force Nizam-ul-Mulk to admit defeat and agree to a peace on terms dictated by the Marathas.

Nizam-ul-Mulk after defeating Mubariz Khan (1st Oct., 1724), took possession of Haidarabad and soon settled down as the master of the six subahs of Mughal Deccan. Thenceforth, though he never renounced his allegiance to the Delhi Emperor, he acted as his own master in every respect. His strong and able rule gave some peace to the country and increased the national wealth. But when he tried to check the Maratha depredations in the name of collecting *chauth*, and to resume possession of the old Mughal villages, illegally seized by them during the past quarter century of war and anarchy in the Deccan, he was resisted by the Maratha barons, and thus war became inevitable.

Dividing Marathas

On his side, Nizam-ul-Mulk revived Aurangzib's old game of weakening the Maratha royal power by seducing to his banners those nobles of King Shahu who were jealous of the Peshwa Baji Rao I, and renewing the civil war in the house of Shivaji—between Shahu of Satara (the son of that great Raja's eldest son) and Shambhuji II of Kolhapur (the son of his younger son, Rajaram). This Shambhuji himself came over to the Nizam's Court with a band of selfish Maratha nobles and pressed Asaf Jah to conquer Shahu's dominions for him. An army was raised near Aurangabad for the projected invasion of Poona, which was due to start in November, 1727, at the end of the rainy season.

Baji Rao learnt of the plot very early and struck the first blow. With a force (about 6,000 strong), composed entirely of light cavalry, without guns, carts, baggage or camp bazar, he raided Asaf Jah's territory, moving with incredible rapidity and living off the country. He never stood anywhere to give battle, but only spread fire and plunder on the two sides of his path.

Crossing the Godavari near Puntamba on 17th October, the Peshwa burst into Asaf Jah's territory on the north bank, and skirting the larger cities like Baizapur and Aurangabad some distance on their west and north, he raided the Jalna and Sindhkhed districts, sacking and burning, till he arrived near Jafarabad (on the Purna river, 9 miles south-east of the famous battlefield of Assaye) on 3rd November. But his roving bands when dispersed for plunder were caught up and given a severe beating by Nizam's ablest lieutenant Iwaz Khan on 6th November in the Jalna district.

We next find Baji Rao resting and recouping his army at Deulghat, 25 miles north-east of Jafarabad, till the beginning of December. But on the 2nd of that month he was on the move again, and made an unexpected dash eastwards, *via* Narsi to Basim in north Berar (8th December) and Mangrul of the Pirs, 25 miles north-east of that town (the next day). Then suddenly changing his direction he turned north for 50 miles to Hadgaon (on the 10th) and next due west into East Khandesh, threatening Nizam's base of Burhanpur—from the south (15th December).

Nowhere was the Maratha leader's progress arrested. Avoiding pitched battles, he began a series of bewilderingly rapid marches which completely baffled and exhausted his enemy. In fact, in this cross-country race over a vast broken country, Nizam with his mail-clad heavy cavalry and cumbrous artillery, was out-manoeuvred by the Maratha light horse and toiled painfully behind it, without being able to prevent its ravages, or to bring it to action. Nizam's vanguard under Iwaz Khan followed the Marathas, with their master coming up one stage behind as a support. The Muslims were utterly exhausted by the hardships and privation of this waterless tract, and Nizam gave up the pursuit after reaching a few miles beyond Burhanpur, and halted to refresh his troops.

Baji Rao now burst into Gujrat, which province was not included in Nizam's charge. Crossing the Tapti river some distance west of Chopra (24th Dec.) and the Narmada at the Baba Piara ford, 30 miles south of Baroda (3rd January, 1728), south to Songad fort, 85 miles south of Baroda and 45 miles due east of Surat (12th January). Here he passed 12 days.

In the meantime Nizam-ul-Mulk had learnt at Burhanpur about Baji Rao's exact position, and resumed the chase after him. Arriving near Surat by long marches, he encamped. Baji Rao being thus cut off from the western or sea-side region with its rich towns, darted in the north-eastern direction, to the Ali-Mohan (Chota Udaipur) country, reaching Panwad, 80 miles north-east of Songad on 31st January.

Nizam Captures Poona

Nizam, losing sight of his enemy, and worn out by his long and fruitless marches, wisely changed his plan of campaign. Giving up the pursuit of the elusive Baji Rao, he in full force entered the Poona district, now denuded of its defenders. No resistance could be made; Raja Shahu and his Court took refuge in Purandar fort; every military station and town in the Poona district submitted to Nizam in terror and was placed in charge of some agent of the Kolhapur Raja. Finally Nizam entered Poona city, proclaimed Shambhuji's authority over the country and celebrated the Raja's marriage with a princess of Ramnagar.

Meantime, Baji Rao after roaming in the Ali-Mohan country, was induced by Udaji Pawar to go to Kuksi, 25 miles east of Ali (10th February), and thence turned homewards, going 80 miles south to Betavad, 15 miles north-west of Amalner, in West Khandesh (13th February). Here he received frantic appeals from Raja Shahu to come back for the defence of the Maratha homeland and capital. But with unfailing foresight Baji Rao planned the automatic evacuation of the Poona district by threatening the enemy's capital. Instead of going to Poona he turned south-east and crossing the Ajanta range by the Kesari ghat, burst into the Gandapur and Baizapur districts, west of Nizam's capital Aurangabad, pillaging and burning. Nizam-ul-Mulk at once withdrew from Poona with all his troops, deposited his camp and baggage in Ahmadnagar fort, and then on 24th February set out in light marching order to overtake Baji Rao, who had reached Palkhed, 12 miles east of Baizapur and 28 miles west of Aurangabad on the 25th. For the next six days "Baji Rao plundered on both flanks of the Nizam's line of advance, prevented the coming of provisions, and wherever a ravine or stream crossed the path of the Deccani army he used to attack them, but when fighting began he took to flight and engaged in Cossack-like tactics." At last the Nizam was manoeuvred into a broken waterless ground and completely hemmed in. However, after undergoing unspeakable hardship, he cut his way out, but in utter disgust gave up the plan of supporting Shambhuji II. By the treaty of Shevgaon (12 March), he conceded all the Maratha claims.

The military student of this campaign will find his task easier, if he takes a large map of the Deccan plateau (Degree sheets) and pins a flag on each stage of the Maratha army's march. This campaign gives a classic example of what the predatory horse, when led by a genius, could achieve in the age before light artillery.

Baji Rao's Route

1727

13-14 Oct. in Pargana Parner, about 50 miles north-east of Puna.

17 Oct. Pantamba, 50 m. north of Parner on the south bank of the Godavari.

18-20 Oct. Andar-sul, 18 m. n. of Pantamba and on the n. bank of the Goda.

22 Oct. Near Yeole, 9 m. n. w. of Andar-sul.

23 Oct. Borsar, 10 m. n. e. of Baizapur.

24 Oct. Dhamangaon, 4 m. n. of Takli city and 8 m. n. e. of Elora.

28 Oct. Ridhere in pargana Dabhade (Dabhade is 18 miles n. w. of Jalna).

29 Oct. Dongar-gaon Dabhade, 2 m. n. e. of Dabhade.

30 Oct. Pangri, 8 m. n. w. of Jalna and 10 m. s. e. of Dabhade.

2 Nov. Palaskhed pargana, in Sindhkhed district, 20 m. n. of Jalna and 9 m. s. w. of Jafarabad.

3 Nov. Near Jafarabad, 9 m. s. e. of Assaye battlefield.

6 Nov. Battle in Jalna district. Baji defeated.
1 Dec. Halt at Deulghat, 5 miles s. w. of Buldana.
3 Dec. Manbad, near Pathri.
4 Dec. On the river Purna, near Parli. There is a *Padali*, 16 m. s. of Lonar lake and on the Purna R.
5 Dec. Halt near Avta Nagnath (=Nagthan) 7 m. s. w. of Basim.
6 Dec. City of Narsi, 25 m. s. of Basim.
8 Dec. Near Basim in Berar province.
9 Dec. near Mangrul of the Pir, 25 m. n. e. of Basim.
10 Dec. Hadgaon, 50 m. n. of Mangrul.
12th Dec. Wankhed, 12 m. n. w. of Panchgovan.
13 Dec. Near Zahut? (probably *Jamod*), 15 m. n. w. of Wankhed.
15 Dec. Province of Zainabad (Burhanpur south).
17 Dec. Adavad, 11 m. e. of Chopra in West Khandesh.
18 Dec. Kusumba, 12 m. w. of Dhulia.
19 Dec. On Tapti bank, in Nandurbar dist.
23 Dec. Bhadvad, 12 m. s. w. of Nandurbar.
24 Dec. On Tapti bank.
25 Dec. Kukar-munda, 12 m. n. of Nandurbar, but on the north bank of the Tapti.

1728

3-4 Jan. Narmada bank at the Baba Piyara ford, 30 m. s. of Baroda, and 8 m. n. of Nandod (Rajpipla Rd. Ry. station).
6-8 Jan. Panetha, on the south bank of the Narmada, 14 m. n. e. of Shuklatirth.
10 Jan. Ten Talav, 20 m. n. e. of Panetha but on the north bank of the Narmada.
12-24 Jan. Near Songad, 80 m. s. of Baroda, and midway on the Surat-Nandurbar Ry. line. Mohan city is 70 m. n. e. of it. Udaji Pawar interviews Baji here on 24th January.
31 Jan. Panwad, pargana Mohan, 10 m. n. of Mohan.
2 Feb. Tanbhala, pargana Mohan, 20 m. n. e. of Nandod Ry. station.

3 Feb. Jambli? pargana Mohan (probably Jhalambi, 22 m. e. of Songad).
5 Feb. District of Ali. Ali city is 20 m. n. e. of Mohan, and 20 m. e. of Chota Udaipur, which is 50 m. e. of Baroda.
10 Feb. Kuksi, 25 m. due e. of Ali.
13-14 Feb. Betavad, 80 m. s. of Kuksi but across a very hilly tract and 15 m. n. w. of Amalner in W. Khandesh.
16 Feb. Mukti, district Dhulia, 10 m. e. of Dhulia City.
25 Feb. Near Palkhed, 12 m. e. of Baizapur.
March 2. Crosses the Godavari, to the south bank, at Kalegaon, 18 m. e. of Nevasa.
March 11. Shevgaon district, on the Goda south bank.
March 12. Treaty of Shevgaon, signed at Lakhephul, 6 m. w. of Paithan.

Chapter XXI

ARMY OF THE MUGHAL EMPERORS

The military organisation of the Emperors of Delhi came in time to be imitated, more or less, by all the other Powers in India with local variations due to race, terrain and State income. It was Turkish in its origin and retained the Turkish character and words to the end, though a rapid decline overtook it on the Indian soil.

Its most remarkable characteristic was that in its pristine purity it harnessed the rude vigour of the nomads of the prairies to a highly intellectual organisation, guided at the top by the most civilised of the Asiatic races, the Persians. India's wealth enabled the Delhi Emperors to expand the civil side of the Army so vastly as in the end to smother the fighting force under its weight and turn the State bankrupt. Non-combatants outnumbered the actual fighters as ten to one. The necessary presence of spies, news-writers, clerks, account-keepers, suppliers of provisions and comforts, and transport agents, besides moving *bazars* and owners of hired carts and camels, as well as money-lenders accompanying their debtors, at last brought the army to a standstill, but it was a machine worked by educated men.

In its best days the imperial army proved its efficiency against Asiatic foes by its superior organisation and discipline. The troops did not form a wild multitude like a herd of 10,000 or 20,000 bisons rushing through the American prairies. They were divided into distinct groups, each under its separate commander, holding its allotted place in a duly graded series of ranks from a company to an army division. When led by a strong and able sovereign personally present in the field, this habit of discipline and co-operation with other parts, gave the imperial army an inestimable advantage, when compared with the hordes of clan levies of the Hindus; each little platoon of it could silently take up its position in the line and it could be shifted to a new place in the field with any change in the tide of combat, smoothly and promptly like the pawns on a chess-board. Indeed, the Persian historians are fond of calling war a game of chess!

Battle formation

The battle formation of the Turks, brought to India by the dynasty of Babur, was scientific, clear-cut and effective till in later days luxury and excessive numbers ruined the entire machine. There was first, a strong vanguard of specially selected brave and well-equipped troops, with artillery, before whom spread a loose screen of skirmishers (horse-archers) without fire arms, advancing and falling back, without disordering the vanguard, but skirting its flanks to the rear, if driven hard. Behind the vanguard came the main army,—Left Wing, Centre (the strongest in number of men and officers, and inspired by the supreme commander's presence), and Right Wing. And finally stood the rear-guard or more correctly Reserve (which was distinct from the baggage-guard). This simple arrangement was later on further improved by adding detached flank corps to each Wing and the Centre, when the total rose to unmanageable numbers.

From the first, the Turks had two smaller and very mobile bodies, called the *iltmish* (which I translate as the advanced reserve or commando troops). These were stationed just at the shoulders of the Centre and could be pushed very promptly to the support of any hard-pressed section of the front. In the early days of Central Asian warfare, these two select cavalry corps acted as the enveloping agent; they were employed in turning the enemy's flanks and closing in his rear "like the horns of a crescent."

A good distance behind the line of battle lay the camp, with an escort, who did not join in the fight, unless the enemy made a detour and attacked the camp.

It should be remembered that in the 17th century the big artillery was too unwieldy to be moved during a battle, and it could fire only once in half an hour; so that it lay inactive on the ground after the first discharge (from a distance) was over and the men clashed together.

For a picture of the miserable condition of the Mughal army in its last days and its causes, the best source is William Irvine's Army of the Indian Moghuls, (Luzac & Co. 1903), pp. 296-300.

Army personnel vastly expanded

Akbar's reign as Emperor of India (1556-1605) introduced a revolutionary change in the character and organisation of the Delhi armies and its effect was to give a new shape to Indian warfare. The end of Shah Jahan's reign (1657) shows the new-system in its fully developed and universal form. The change followed two lines,—first the State armies became vaster in size and more complicated in their organisation than before, because they were now the agents of very large and rich empires, commanding boundless resources of men and money; and secondly, gunpowder began to dominate the field.

A necessary corollary of the second factor was the large-scale employment of a foreign element,—at first pure-blooded Europeans and latterly Indo-European half breeds,—who ultimately dominated the fire-arms department, degrading the Indian artillerymen to a subordinate position and influence in battles.

The change in the character of the Mughal Army showed itself fully in the reign of Shah Jahan (1628-1658), though its seed was sown by Akbar. The Empire of Delhi had now become a very vast dominion, covering more than half the Indian continent and embracing its richest lands and ports and yielding a revenue of more than 12 crores of rupees a year. Thus, the twelve thousand horsemen with whom Babur had conquered the throne of Delhi in 1526 were a century after him replaced by a fighting force five or six times as large. Taking fort-garrisons, provincial troops, and *sehbandi* (or militia for helping revenue collectors) along with the regular army, Shah Jahan did not exaggerate when he mourned on his fall from the throne (in 1658), "Yesterday I was the master of nine lakhs of troopers". The commissioned officers (called *mansabdars*) on his army-roll numbered 8,000 in the year 1647.

Causes of decline

This vast and costly army naturally became a cumbrous machine moving very slowly. The fighting force was followed by a horde of civilians, clerks, accountants, spies, news-reporters, couriers, contractors, shop-keepers, dancing girls and even *faquirs*, till the non-combatants outnumbered the soldiers by ten to one. The imperial army became incapable of making lightning raids, night attacks or ambuscades, such as Babur's Turks had so well carried out and Ahmad Shah Durrani's troops were to do in the 18th century. We can easily see why the Delhi Army failed against the Marathas in the Deccan and Nadir Shah in Hindustan under the later Mughals.

The countless departments under which the military administration was divided only increased red tape and delay in the execution of any order, while the vast amount of material and comforts which had become necessary caused the transport to break down in the midst of a campaign. In its best days the Imperial Army could not be defeated in a pitched battle, it could only be starved out of a post. It moved like a huge road-roller, which was sure to be bogged in the marshes of Assam or the broken rocky soil of the Deccan, where it could not move or even survive for want of food. The imperial camp has been aptly described by a European traveller as a moving city, it could not live off the country like Babur's swift hardy horsemen.

A sickening picture of the degeneracy of the Mughal Army, 143 years after Akbar's death, is presented by the story of the march of the Emperor Muhammad Shah's army from Delhi to oppose Ahmad Shah Durrani at Manupur (1748). For a full description based on the eye-witness Anandram's reports, see my *Fall of the Mughal Empire*, Vol. I, Ch. 5 & 12. This vast assembly of more than two lakhs of men was in effect a city of tents, which advanced two miles in one day, then halted for two or three days to take breath! This was not war.

This inflation of the Imperial Army sapped its vigour in another way also. Such vast numbers of men and transport animals and enormous quantities of material ate up a year's revenue of the State. Hence the soldiers' pay fell into arrears, which in the last days accumulated for three years or even longer, and the starving soldiers were in a chronic state of mutiny, imprisoning or assaulting their officers and refusing to make a start when a campaign was ordered, unless their dues were paid and a bounty advanced for feeding their families during their absence. Our national fighting machine lost all its efficiency.

Artillery improvements in 17th Century

Babur's fire-arms were worked by Asiatic Muslims who had been trained in the service of the Sultans of Turkey (whence their title of Rumi, from Constantinople which was called the Eastern Rome). He and his successors also employed Shias of Persia, who had learned this art at second hand through war with the Turks of Asia Minor. In Akbar's reign a radical change was effected in this arm. His conquest of Gujrat brought him into direct contact with the Portuguese of Goa and his religious toleration and kindness to Catholic monks created a link between him and the Government of Portugal, by which many Portuguese and more half-caste gunners were induced to enter his service. His conquest of Bengal increased his artillery personnel by the enrolment of Feringi mercenaries who had formerly served the independent Bengal Sultans and now joined him for a livelihood. Thus the Rumi and Persian gunners were gradually replaced by Feringis.

In the middle of the 17th century came a still greater change. Military adventurers of pure European blood from France and England began to flock directly to the Mughal Court, and not through Goa as before. The Thirty Years' War on the Continent (1618-1648) in its closing years threw vast numbers of European soldiers into the streets as paupers. And the growth of the seaborne trade with India in consequence of the establishment of the Dutch, English and French East India Companies, made it easy for European adventurers to come to our fabled land of gold, as sailors or soldiers on board the India-bound merchant vessels, desert their ships at some Indian port and proceed to the court of some Indian prince to make their fortune in his military service. Thus, Niccolao Manucci, an Italian lad of fourteen, came to India in 1656 as a stow-away. In the 18th century the Frenchmen Rene Madec and C. Perron and the Irishman George Thomas were examples of such run-away sailors who rose to be Nabobs.

Another channel of recruitment for Europeans was also opened. The Safavi dynasty of Persian Shahs, early in the 17th century, welcomed and patronised Europeans (mostly French and English), and many adventurers of these two races found in Persia a very convenient halfway house to India. Thus Goa fell into neglect as a supply-centre of European gunners for the Mughal service.

The result of this foreign recruitment was that the technical leadership of the Mughal artillery department passed into Christian hands,—a few pure-blooded and trained Europeans at the top, many mestizoes under them, and a long tail of pure Indian Christians at the bottom. These last were called *topases* (a corruption of the Turki word *top-chi* or gunner) and were held in deserved contempt.

The development of the firearms themselves was also remarkable. The first artillery consisted of tubes clamped to short wooden beams; these beams were transported by being loaded like logs in ordinary carts, unloaded on the battle-field and placed immovable each in its appointed position. Guns mounted each on a wheeled carriage of its own, were later introduced from Europe, and this convenient device was adopted in the Mughal Army by Akbar. Wheels made the ordnance lighter and more mobile, and thus the element of surprise in the concentration and shifting of fire-power became possible. The improved range and accuracy of musket-fire since Babur's time and also the greater mobility of wheeled cannon, greatly increased the danger to the commanders who used to ride to battle on the tallest elephants in order to be able to survey the whole field and also cheer their troops by making themselves visible to them. The deadly effect of the improved cannon was clearly proved at the battle of Jajau (1707), where all the leaders on one side, Prince Muhammad Azam, his son Bidar Bakht, his Rajput general Dalpat Rao Bundela, were shot down and a crushing defeat inflicted. So also, at Shakar Khera

(1724), Mubariz Khan and his two sons and at Gheria (1740) the Nawab Sarfaraz Khan were brought down by the enemy's gunners, and the defeat of their side was the immediate result.

With the increase in the mobility and range of artillery, it became necessary for the general to use telescopes for learning the exact situation of their troops. But the first use of a field-glass by an Indian commander recorded in history is that of Najib-ud-daula during Jawahir Singh Jat's attack on Delhi in 1764, and the next that of Mahadji Sindhia during the Lalsot campaign of 1787. (See my *Fall of the Mughal Empire*, Vol. II, Ch. 23 and Vol. III, Ch. 35).

Muskets were also greatly improved as the result of the constant care of the Emperor Akbar and imitation of the latest models imported from Europe. In consequence of this, increase in the power of hand-guns, musketeers (*barqandazes*) began to dominate the infantry arm and ultimately displaced the foot soldiery armed with sword and spear, in the Mughal army.

Races employed in the artillery arm

Europeans were preferred in the artillery department on account of their proved superiority in marksmanship and alertness. Our cannon-founders at first were ex-servants of the Osmanli Turks from Asia Minor, but in the late 18th century a superior kind of artillery was cast for our Mughal and Maratha rulers only by Frenchmen and Britons, such as Le Vassoult, Sangster, Perron and others. The Indian gun-founders could produce only clumsy primitive ordnance. But the clever Indian smiths could successfully imitate the best European muskets, and this industry remained in Indian hands, till the invention of rifled breech-loaders in the middle of the 19th century. These Agra and Mungir gunsmiths of Indian race excited the admiration of British officers by their clever imitation of European models as late as the age of Waterloo.

All the firearms of the Mughal army formed a separate department under one chief, styled the *Mir Atish* or *Darogha-i-Top-Khanah*, and no part of it was under any infantry colonel. The department was divided into two branches, each with its separate arsenal and administrative staff, but a common head.

One was called the *Jinsi-topkhanah* and comprised the wheeled artillery, the fort-guns and the swivel-guns; the other was called the *Dasti-topkhanah* and dealt with the muskets or hand-guns. In the artillery proper, Europeans, mestizoes and black Christians predominated, the low-caste Hindus and Muslims supplying only the gun lascars, though dignified with the title of *Golandaz.* In the hand-gun branch most of the captains (called *hazaris*) and men were Hindus of Oudh and Buxar, but many were foreign Muslims from Persia (hence called Mughalia) and some Indo-Muslims of the Ruhela and other Afghan clans (especially from Malwa and Sindh).

Thus, the Hindus were totally eliminated from the main artillery department of the Mughal Army, which was officered and manned mostly by foreigners.

In the Indian armies the cavalry did not carry carbines, but only swords and lances, all the musketeers were unmounted infantry. But in the late 18th century, the Sikh *misls* and the Durrani troops used fire-arms from horseback and camel-back as a rule, and thus restored the element of mobility to Indian warfare. Still later, this tendency was counteracted by the increased importance of European-trained infantry or "campoo paltans" which necessarily robbed the "regular" armies of swiftness of movement.

We should bear in mind that in the Mughal artillery guns were drawn by bullocks, with an elephant in some cases to push big ordnance from behind on broken roads. This was also the practice of the E. I. Co. to the end of the 18th century, though in Europe wheeled artillery was drawn by horses from about 1600. It was only in 1793 that De Boigne attached four light pieces (three pounders, called gallopers) each drawn by two horses to the regular Cavalry Regiment raised by him for Mahadji Sindhia while the bigger pieces of the force were ox-drawn. The munition for each galloper was carried by four camels into the field. The British used "the Flying Artillery" or horse-drawn galloper guns (6 lbs.) for the first time in General Lake's North Indian campaign against the Marathas in 1803, with great success. (See *Fall of The Mughal Empire,* IV, 117, 269, 283, 293).

J. Forbes wrote in 1775,—"The war-rocket used by the

Marathas is composed of an iron tube eight or ten inches long, and near two inches in diameter; this destructive weapon is sometimes fixed to a rod of iron, sometimes to a straight two-edged sword, but most commonly to a strong bamboo-cane, four or five feet long, with an iron spike projecting beyond the tube: to this rod or staff, the tube filled with combustible materials is fastened, and on the lighted match setting fire to the fuse, is projected with great velocity; if well directed, which is an uncertain operation, it causes much confusion and dismay among the enemy." (*Oriental Memoirs*, 2nd ed., i. 359-360).

Appendix I

MARATHA SYSTEM OF WAR

The Maratha type of warfare had certain peculiarities which were the natural consequences of their country and race. The Deccan land is dry and broken, being cut up into many small compartments by hill-spurs and deep stony-bedded rivers. The people were a frugal hardy high-spirited race, mostly peasants, habituated to self-government in their village-communities; hence they supplied a type of soldiers quite different from the armed retainers of rich and luxurious kingdoms who received costly equipment and elaborate training in standing camps.

The first characteristic of the Maratha armies was their extreme mobility. The reason was that they were all horsemen, often with one spare horse for each trooper, and they were not encumbered with baggage or tents, as they lived off the country and their hardy ponies fed on the wayside shrubs. They had no artillery, no workshop, no camp-servants. The Pindharis who formed a regular appendage to the Maratha armies, were not attendants on the fighting men, but looters, pure and simple; they were all mounted men and relieved the regular cavalry of some tasks like reconnoitring, causing distraction to the enemy by attacking his baggage in the rear, while the soldiers were busy fighting in front, and usually the pursuit and plunder of a defeated enemy, while their own regular troops were too fatigued after the battle.

A French officer gives this picture of the great Shivaji's army during his invasion of the Madras Coast in 1677:—

> "The camp of Shivaji is without pomp, without women, and without baggage. It has only two tents, both of simple coarse stuff and very small,—one of them for himself and the other for his Prime Minister. There are ordinarily three horses to every two men, which contributes to the speed that he makes, he thus surprises his enemies

who believe him to be far distant when he falls upon them."

The early Maratha army is thus described by Mons. Francois Martin, the founder of Pondicherry, who saw it in Jinji, where Shivaji's son Rajaram was holding court in December 1692:

"The Maratha standing army consists of 1,50,000 horsemen. Their ordinary arms are the half-lance and the sabre for the offensive and the round shield for defence. Some have bows and arrows, but few. The Muslims have this advantage over the Marathas that besides the musketeers whom they have in their cavalry, the bows and arrows which they use, ordinarily and by preference, are better than their enemy's and stop the Marathas from a distance. The Muslims are also better soldiers; a thousand of their bowmen will not retreat before a body of three or four thousand Maratha cavaliers, or even more. The Marathas are good in making surprises, in which they succeed, being men capable of bearing fatigue, contented with little, and carrying no retinue or baggage."

A sorry picture of the latter-day Maratha army under the Peshwas is given by J. Forbes (1775) in his 'Oriental Memoirs and Dirom (1791) in his Narrative of the Campaign in India.

The austere simplicity of the Maratha chief is also illustrated by the portrait of Baji Rao I which an Indian artist drew at the command of the Nizam Asaf Jah. Muslim nobles are usually portrayed as sitting gorgeously dressed in a chair and smelling at a rose, held in the right hand, while servants, standing behind, are fanning them. But Asaf Jah had asked for a picture of Baji Rao 'exactly' as he lived, and the artist drew the great conquering Peshwa as sitting on horseback, dressed like a common trooper and squeezing some dry peas in the palm of his left hand before chewing them: That was the supreme Maratha general in camp.

The speed of the Maratha armies aroused in their enemies' minds equal terror and astonishment. The Maratha troops that raided Bengal from 1742 onwards are thus described by a Bengali Brahman of the time!

"Rajah Shahu's troops created a local cataclysm

(*pralaya*) and extirpated the people of the Bengal villages ....In one day they can cover a hundred leagues.... They rob all the property and abduct the women. If it comes to a battle they secretly flee away to some other province. Their main strength lies in their marvellously swift horses." (Vaneshwar Vidyalankar).

Enveloping Tactics

The second characteristic of Maratha warfare was that they always pursued enveloping tactics, intended to harass their enemy and cut off his supplies. They would not offer a stand-up fight nor go forth to a pitched battle in reply to a formal challenge, as was the Rajput practice. Hence, the Maratha army was called by the North Indian people *ghanimi fauj* or predatory horse, like the light forayers of Scotland. A Muslim historian has given a fanciful etymology to the word *Marhatta* by saying that it was short for *Mar ke hat jata*, that is, "they strike a blow and immediately flee away." This is only a half truth, because the Marathas under able leadership have been known to stand up and fight when the odds were not against them.

The efficiency of the Maratha system lay in this that their vast hordes of horsemen could march long distances with extreme speed and secrecy, disperse for foraging or bewildering their enemy, and yet combine for striking a blow. This mobility also enabled them to break off engagement at any time they chose and vanish to a safe distance, without giving their enemy a chance of crushing them by pursuit. Shivaji's tactics at the battle of Dindori (Oct. 1670) gave a classic example of it.

So long as the armament and system of war were simple and the country fertile, these peculiar Maratha tactics could succeed. Against walled cities, fully provisioned or camps guarded by artillery, they were powerless for attack, though they could starve out such defended posts by cutting off their supplies. Sudden surprise of an unprepared enemy by vast bodies of light cavalry,—called in the Persian histories as "more numerous than ants and locusts",—and complete envelopment of his position, was the secret of success of the Maratha system of warfare. And yet the Marathas themselves gave instances of gross carelessness and failure to keep watch in their own camps.

Witness how the great Shivaji was all but caught by Ranmast Khan when returning from the loot of Jalna (1679), how the triumphant Bhaskar Pandit's camp at Katwa was beaten up by Alivardi Khan in 1742, and how Bussy surprised the great Peshwa Balaji Baji in 1751, between Arangaon and Sarola on the Sina at night when taking his bath during a lunar eclipse. Govind Ballal Bundele was surprised and killed by the Durrani General Atai Khan at Jalalabad in broad daylight, (17th Dec., 1760) and the great Malhar Rao Holkar himself was put to a hurried flight by the same enemy near Sikandarabad (4th March, 1760).

At Its Best

The invasions of North-India under Baji Rao I and his sons, in the first half of the 18th century show the Maratha system at its best, because there was as yet no multiplication of departments and increase of stores and *material* to destroy speed. We must bear in mind that the battle of Panipat in 1761 was in no sense a typical Maratha battle. Nor did Mahadji Sindhia's famous victories over the Rajputs (in 1790) and Daulat Rao Sindhia's battles with Lake and Wellington (in 1803) illustrated the Maratha system of war. They were really fought by modern-trained battalions of Oudh men (like the E. I. Company's sepoys of the Bengal Army), only serving a Maratha pay-master.

In fact, firearms could not be fitted into the Maratha system of war, and as the 18th century neared its end, firepower began to dominate the battle-fields of India, from the improved arms and more efficient foreign teachers borrowed from Europe. To what depth of inefficiency and degradation the national army of the Marathas could sink when the old "light foray" tactics had become out of date and yet the European system could not be learnt, is best illustrated by Major Dirom's picture of the Peshwa's army under Parashuram Bhau Patwardhan and Hari Pant Phadke that came to co-operate with Lord

Cornwallis in the war with Tipu Sultan in May 1791. He writes: —

> "The park of artillery, where all their guns are collected, made an extraordinary appearance. The gun-carriages, in which they trust to the solidity of the timber and use but little iron in their construction, are clumsy beyond belief; particularly the wheels which are low and formed of large solid pieces of wood united. The guns are of all sorts and dimensions.... (They are mostly venerated for their ancient services, but now unfit for use). Were the guns even serviceable, the small supply of ammunition with which they are provided has always effectively prevented the Maratha artillery from being formidable to their enemies.... There are sometimes 100 or 150 bullocks in a string of pairs, to one gun.
>
> "The Maratha infantry (of the paltan) is composed of black Christians and despicable poor wretches of the lowest caste, . . . their muskets are neither clean nor complete; and few are provided with either ammunition or accoutrements. They are commanded by half-caste people of Portuguese and French extraction.... The Marathas do not appear to treat their infantry with more respect than they deserve, as they ride through them without any ceremony on the march." ('Narrative of Campaign', pp. 10-11).

Santaji Ghorpare Crushes Qasim Khan, November, 1695

The classic example of the early Maratha type of warfare is supplied by Santaji Ghorpare (who died in 1697). He was a perfect master of this art, which can be more correctly described as Parthian warfare than as guerilla tactics, because he could not only make night marches and surprises, but also cover long distances quickly and combine the movements of large bodies over wide areas with an accuracy and punctuality which were incredible in any Asiatic army other than those of Zengis Khan and Timur. Santaji had an inborn genius for handling large bodies of troops spread through long distances, changing his tactics so as to take prompt advantage of every change in the enemy's plans and condition, and organising combined movements without the risk of failure. The success of his tactics depended on the rapid movement of his troops and on his subordinates carrying out his orders punctually to the minute. He, therefore, insisted on implicit obedience from his officers, and enforced the strictest discipline in his army by the severest punishments.

While the Maratha King Rajaram was besieged in the hill fort of Jinji (near Pondicherry) by the Mughal General Zulfiqar Khan and Aurangzib was conquering places in the Maratha homeland in Western India, Santaji made a diversion for his Rajah by plundering the Mughal province of Bijapur; then in October, 1695, he turned southwards to convey his rich store of booty to his own estate in the Bellary district. The Mughal Emperor from his base, some two hundred miles in the north, ordered Qasim Khan, his Governor of Sera (western Mysore) to intercept the raider. From his own camp he detached Khanazad Khan and some others of his highest younger officers to reinforce Qasim Khan, with 4,800 troopers, chosen from the imperial guards and personal retinue and the Court nobles' contingents. They joined Qasim Khan about 12 miles from the Marathas' expected track, early in November.

Santaji learnt of it when at a distance. He came up with the imperialists by swift marches, and skilfully matured a plan for their destruction which the luxury and thoughtlessness of the Mughal general crowned with the most complete success imaginable. Qasim Khan, in order to do honour to his high-born and influential courtier guests, discarded the austere camp equipage of a general who would wage war with the Marathas wisely, and brought out of his stores in Adoni fort costly articles and furniture such as splendid decorated tents, gold and silver vessels and China ware, and sent them six miles ahead of that night's halting place, to be kept ready for himself and his guests when they would arrive there at the end of the next day's march.

Learning of his enemy's folly, Santa showed the highest tactical power in making his dispositions so as to take the utmost advantage of their mistake. He divided his army into three bodies of which one was sent to plunder the Mughal advanced camp, another to fight the soldiers marching six miles behind it, and the third was held in reserve ready for action at any point required. Barmappa Naik, the Berad zamindar of Chittaldurg district, now joined the Marathas in hope of a share of the spoils, and thus the imperialists were ringed round by enemies and cut off from all local information or guidance.

An hour and a half after sunrise next day, the first Maratha division fell upon Qasim Khan's tents, pitched six miles to the front the day before, slew the guards and carried off everything they could, setting fire to the heavy tents. Qasim Khan on hearing of it, hurried towards the point of attack. Before he had gone two miles, the second division of Santa intercepted him and a battle began. The enemy's numbers were overwhelming, and they had a very large corps of *Kala-piada* musketeers, the best marksmen among the Kanarese tribes, in addition to the countless Maratha light horse. While this battle was raging with heavy slaughter on both sides, the reserve division of Santa's army attacked the camp and baggage left behind where the Mughals had passed the night before.

This news reached Qasim Khan and Khanazad Khan in the heat of the battle and it shook their firmness. So, they broke off engagement and retreated to Dodderi, 96 miles south of Adoni, in a straight line.

Dodderi is a small walled fort with a large tank of water south of it. The two Khans encamped outside. As the night closed, the Marathas completely encircled them. For the first three days the enemy only showed themselves at a distance without fighting, till some thousands of foot-musketeers sent by Barmappa Naik joined them, when, on the fourth day they delivered an attack. The imperial artillery munitions had been plundered in their rear camp and the little store with the field army was soon exhausted. So, the Khans' soldiers sat down in despair, as a helpless target for the Kanarese marksmen. Fully one-third of the Mughal force had been slain in the two camps, during the retreat, and on the bank of the tank at Dodderi.

The Muslim soldiers now faced utter starvation. Their two Generals sneaked into the fort at night, leaving their men to their fate outside it. Qasim Khan was a habitual opium-eater and the lack of the drug caused his death on the third day. At last, Khanazad Khan in utter helplessness capitulated to Santa, and secured his release by promising a ransom of 20 lakhs of rupees and giving up all the treasure, animals and other property of the doomed army, on the 13th day after his entering the fort, (early in December).

In the meantime, Aurangzib had deputed another very high General, Himmat Khan, to co-operate with Qasim Khan. This officer, on account of the smallness of his force had shut himself up in Basavapatan, 40 miles west of Dodderi. On 20th January, 1696, Santa appeared before Himmat Khan's post at the head of 10,000 cavalry and nearly the same number of infantry. His Karnataki foot-musketeers occupied a hill overlooking the place. Himmat Khan boldly attacked and dislodged them from it, and then drove his elephant on to attack Santa, when he was shot dead by a bullet in the forehead. His troops were besieged in Basavapatan, but the Marathas withdrew with the captured baggage of the Khan after some days, and the garrison was later relieved by a new imperial detachment.

APPENDIX II

ELEPHANTRY

In our Sanskrit epics and books on polity, the army is likened to a man with four limbs, *chaturanga*, or as in English, four arms. These arms are, chariots, elephants, horsemen and infantry. Among these, the chariots have been discussed in my study of Alexander's battle with Poros in 326 B.C. in a previous Chapter. We have historic evidence of the last use of chariots in war in Kharavela's Daccan campaign (about 170 B.C.). There is no mention of this arm in the inscriptions describing the campaigns of Samudra-gupta (c. 350 A.D.) or of Harshavardhan (c. 625). From this we can conclude that charioteers ceased to be a branch of the fighting forces soon after the beginning of the Christian era.

Next comes the elephant corps. Hindu kings took pride in keeping herds of big elephants in their service and assumed the title of Lord of Elephants, Gajapati, as their inscriptions show. Even the Hellenistic dynasty of Eucratides, Bactrian kings of Kabul, issued coins with the head of an elephant covering their helmets, thus proving that they maintained an elephant corps.

The elephant was used in two ways, as a fighting machine and as a transport agent. In both capacities he was invaluable. It is only the long-range fire-arms of modern times that have killed the elephant as a valued instrument of war, and only recent mechanical transport conquering every difficulty of terrain that has displaced this beast as a means of army supply and transport.

Thus, the elephant has now come to be regarded as a symbol of oriental pomp and effeminacy. Especially, habitual fighters on horseback have nothing but contempt for foes who ride to battle on elephants. This attitude was well expressed by Ahmad Shah Durrani's General, Jahan Khan, during his invasion of India in 1767, when accompanying Najib-ud-daula

Ruhela's son, Zabita Khan, in an expedition against the Sikhs. The Afghan sardar said to his Indian ally, "Your head and body seem to have become very soft. You have been habituated to sitting in *palkis* and on carpets; how can you keep pace with us?" Zabita replied, "I too am an Afghan's son." Then Jahan Khan asked him, "Why then are you taking an elephant with yourself?" Zabita answered, "Wherever there is a river on the way, the General crosses it on the elephant's back."

If the elephant were really an article of oriental pomp, the great General Hannibal would not have carried 37 of these beasts with him from Spain in his invasion of Rome; he safely transported them over the intense cold and snow of the Little Bernard Pass as he crossed the Alps. Mommsen holds that Hannibal's aim was to frighten the hill tribes of southern France on his way, by the sight of these strange African beasts, as they could have carried very little of the necessary provisions of his huge army. The terror inspired by these animals among the ancient Romans is well expressed by Macaulay, in reference to the invasion of south Italy by Pyrrhus, the Greek King of Epirus:

"The Greek shall come against thee,
The conqueror of the East.
Before him stalks to battle
The huge earth-shaking beast,
The beast on whom the castle
With all its guards doth stand,
The beast who hath between his eyes,
The serpent for a hand."

Hence the Latin title of the elephant, *angui-manus,* or snake-handed.

Let us first consider the elephant as a mere carrier, apart from his use as a fighter. Here his virtues are many and in some respects without a parallel. In India he is locally born, easily trained, wonderfully sagacious, proverbially faithful, and cheap to keep as, unlike the horse, his food has not to be carried with him but abounds in the plains and jungles around. He can also boldly face the tiger, though not possessing sharp claws or piercing horns or even the shield-like hide of the rhinoceros.

General Sir Sydney Cotton, who so ably disarmed the sepoys at Peshawar during the Sepoy Mutiny of 1857, goes into raptures in praising the usefulness of the elephant. He writes:—

"Strange as it may appear, there is no beast of burden in the world that can beat an elephant in traversing precipitous mountains, and the author never went without these mortars (5½ lbs. mortars conveyed on elephants, in invading the Afridi country). Of all animals of the creation there are none so intelligent and so useful in military operations in mountains as the elephants, and sufficient value and importance is not attached to them in the British (Indian) services. One elephant can transport over long distances six British soldiers, with arms, ammunition and bedding besides rations.

"They raise heavy guns by simultaneous movements. They can climb on hills where even mules cannot go, and during the operations at Shah Musa Khel, the author continually employed them in supplying the light infantry in extended order, with ball ammunition, when no other animals could have been found to do it, even to the very tops of the mountains." (*Nine Years on the N.W.F., 90-92*).

At the opposite corner of India, in Ochterlony's attack on Makwanpur in Nepal by turning the Bichwa-Khori Pass, elephants were employed in carrying stores up the hills. (See a picture in Prinsep's *Transactions*, 2nd edition.)

Babur hits off the merits and defects of the elephant in a few words of his *Memoirs* (Mrs. Beveridge's trans. i, 485).

In Actual Fighting

Besides his usefulness in dragging guns into the field, one elephant doing the work of fifty gun lascars,—the elephant was extremely valuable in actual fighting in the ancient and middle ages. First, in forming the column (Sanskrit name *vyuha*) arrangement of the troops in a Hindu battle, the elephants served as pillars at regular intervals, between which the infantry and cavalry were drawn up. In the battle on the Jhelum, the elephants of Poros "when seen from a distance presented the appearance of towers" (as Quintus Curitus[1] noted in his *History of Alexander*). In fact, the war elephants, in a combat on a plain, best served the purpose of strengthening the line of battle as vertical posts do in a fence or bastions in a fort wall.

During the actual fighting, the elephant did a signal service by supplying the supreme commander with a lofty but quickly movable seat from which he could watch all parts of the field and issue suitable orders to different corps as the tide of battle changed from time to time. The king (or in his absence the commander-in-chief) seated on the tallest elephant's back, thus served as a visible source of encouragement to his foot and horse spread all over the battle-ground. This practice continued from the time of Poros's battle with Alexander (326 B.C.) to the middle of the 18th century, in the battles of Alivardi and Siraj-ud-daulah. Its disadvantage will be pointed out later.

Fighting elephants with their heads sheathed in brass or steel plates, were used as battering rams—or modern tanks, in smashing the thick wooden gates of forts, in an age when blasting them with gunpowder was unknown or impracticable. But in Indian battles, whether in ancient times or the Mughal period, the chief use of the elephant was as rank-breaker (in Persian, *saf-shikan*). The tallest and strongest elephants in the king's service were trained to be goaded to fury (*mast* in Persian) and driven upon the enemy's line of battle, scattering or trampling down the opposing horsemen and infantry. A horse stampedes on seeing an elephant angrily rushing towards it, though Africans have ridden horses in hunting the lion.

How the charge of infuriated elephants succeeds is well illustrated in Akbar's battles. In 1575 his General Munim Khan fought the Bengal Pathan Sultan Daud Khan Karrani at Tukaroi (in the Medinipur district). The scene is thus described by Abul Fazl:—

'The imperial army had not yet been properly arranged, when Gujar Khan (the Pathan General) advanced with a formidable line of active elephants in front and his daring troops

[1] Also Polyainos,—"The elephants were drawn up within 50 yards of each other, and in those interstices were posted his infantry. So that his front exhibited the appearance of a great wall; the elephants looked like so many towers, and the infantry like the parapet between them."

behind. As the tusks and heads and necks of the elephants were covered with black Yak-tails and the skins of the animals, they produced horror and dismay. The horses of the imperial vanguard were frightened on seeing these extraordinary forms and hearing the terrible cries, and they turned back. Though the riders exerted themselves, they were not successful, and our troops lost their formation.

"Khan Alam was overthrown by an elephant. The Afghans crowded on, and he yielded up his life. When this happened to the leader (of the imperial van), Gujar Khan drove off the whole force and proceeded to the advanced reserve (*iltmish*). As soon as he reached it, it broke.... Then Gujar Khan advanced to attack (Akbar's) centre. The courage of the latter was shaken and the men received the retribution of their cowardice. Some of the leaders stood their ground, but Munim Khan's servants did not behave well and he received many wounds.

"Gujar Khan driving the people before him at last came to the imperial camp (in the rear) and passed through it. Then many of his men dispersed for plunder, ... some Mughal officers rallied a body of men and renewed the fight."

Then came the retribution: Gujar Khan was killed with an arrow and his comrades fled away, in spite of their unbroken success so far! (*Akbarnamah*, Beveridge's trans., iii. 176-178).

At Haldighat (June 1576) there was not this massed charge of a hundred or more elephants, but a single combat between the champion elephants of Maharana Pratap Singh and Akbar's General Man Singh; the strength of both sides lay in cavalry and archers. Akbar's official historian thus describes the scene:—

"The enemy's right wing drove off the left wing of the imperialists and their vanguard also prevailed (over ours). Their left wing also overcame the imperial right. As the men (*i.e.* cavalry) did wonders, so also did the elephants perform marvels. On the side of the enemy was the rank-breaking Lona. Our faujdar Jamal Khan brought the elephant Gajmukut to encounter him. The shock of encounter between these two mountain-like forms threw the soldiers into trepidation, and the imperial elephant was wounded and about to fly, when by the

Emperor's good fortune a bullet struck the driver of the enemy's elephant and he turned back.

"Just then a kinsman of the Rana brought forward Ram Prasad, which was the chief elephant on the enemy's side and threw down many of our gallant men. At this time of wavering, Kamal Khan brought up the elephant Gaj-raj and took part in the fight. Panju brought up the elephant Ran Madar opposite Ram Prasad and did exceedingly well. By the strength of the Emperor's fortune, the driver of Ram Prasad was killed by an arrow, and that noted elephant became entered among the spoils (that fell into the hands of the victorious Mughals)." (*Akbarnamah*, iii. 245-246.)

But the use of the elephant in battle had an incurable disadvantage too. The king (or his general) seated on the tallest elephant, presented a conspicuous target to the enemy's gunners or even to Turki horsemen whirling round him on swift horses. If the king was hit or found some reason to dismount from that elephant and take horse, his empty *howda* at once convinced his troops all over the plain that their master was dead and they fled away in panic. Or, if the *mahout* was shot off his seat, the uncontrolled beast would turn round and create the belief that the commander had ordered a general retreat. At the battle of Jajau (1707) Prince Azam Shah and his son Bidar Bakht were shot down on their elephants and at once their armies dispersed in defeat. At the battle of Gheria (1740) Alivardi gained an easy victory when his rival Sarafraz Khan was shot with a bullet on his elephant's back. In the attack on Patna (14th March, 1745) by the rebel general Ghulam Mustafa Khan, when his *mahout* was killed by a musket-shot and that general jumped down from the elephant's back to avoid the danger of being carried away by the uncontrolled beast,—all his troops concluded that their master had been killed and they fled away. Still later in 1756, at Manihari, as soon as Shaukat Jang, the Nawab of Purnia, was shot down from his elephant, opposition ceased at the sight, and the Bengal army had a walk-over up to the enemy's capital.

INDEX

F

G

H

N

O

S

T

U